Candice Brathwaite is a prominent British author and advocate who has made a significant impact with her work on motherhood and diversity. Her *Sunday Times* bestselling book *I Am Not Your Baby Mother* passionately addressed the unique experiences of Black British mothers. Her writing has also appeared in the *Guardian, Harper's Bazaar, Stylist*, the *Huffington Post* and *Grazia*. Candice is a presenter on *Lorraine* and *Steph's Packed Lunch*, and the co-host of the smash-hit podcast, *Closet Confessions*, which has amassed 2.5 million downloads and several sell-out live shows in its first year of production. Her holistic and exuberant online content, which spans from heartfelt wisdom to highly anticipated fashion videos, has gained her a dedicated audience of 290k+ Instagram followers and 370+ on TikTok.

CANDICE BRATHWAITE

MANIFEST

Unlock the Life
You Deserve

QUERCUS

First published in Great Britain in 2024 by Quercus Books

QUERCUS

Quercus Editions Ltd
Carmelite House
50 Victoria Embankment
London EC4Y 0DZ

An Hachette UK company

A CIP catalogue record for this book is available
from the British Library

HB ISBN 978-1-52943-561-0
EBOOK ISBN 978-1-52943-562-7

1

Design by Clare Sivell
Typeset Minion Pro by Jouve (UK), Milton Keynes

Printed and bound in Great Britain by Clays Ltd, Elcograf S.p.A.

Papers used by Quercus are from well-managed forests and other responsible sources.

To my darlings, **Essie** and **Richie Rich**,

Magic laughs in the face of logic.

So, when you are exhausted by playing your human hand, submit to Source and remember: your only duty is to remain unrealistic.

With my eternal love,
Mama

CONTENTS

INTRODUCTION

Perhaps it's because since the early 2000s it has felt – thanks to a plethora of things, not least the economy, the pandemic and the ever-present wars, be they on your home soil or your news feed – as though our personal worlds might at any moment combust, the word *manifestation* has been everywhere.

But what is manifestation? In the most simplistic terms, manifestation is the practice of bringing desires into your life through belief. But now is as good a time as ever to emphasise that by far the most important word in that sentence is 'practice'. Manifestation is not a one-and-done process. It only works if you do, by putting elements into practice, over and over again. Only then will the desires that you believe to be possible come into being.

Manifestation works through the law of attraction, commonly known as LOA. That's the idea that energy attracts its likeness. If you want to attract more positivity into your life, that must be the energy you emit. The law of attraction is an integral part of the manifesting process. Once you can master harnessing precise energies, the world is your oyster.

Before manifestation went mainstream, for a long time it felt as though this 'magical' term bubbled beneath the surface – both the word and the practical steps attached to it seemed to be wrapped in an invisibility cloak, visible only to the most hippie-esque of us.

I myself arrived at the manifestation gates beaten and bloodied. Finally ready to surrender, throw in the wet towel of my will and admit that I, alone in my human form, couldn't quite get anything to work in my favour.

Perhaps it's similar for you. Maybe this is the first piece of manifestation material you've ever engaged with, perhaps it's the ninety-first. What I have observed is that not one of us who has found the call of manifestation too loud to ignore has come here with a smile on our faces. We usually arrive here because we have no more cards left to play. We have given life our all, and yet we feel defeated, deflated and downtrodden.

I first came across the law of attraction in 2009, after my father died suddenly following a short bout of the flu. Less than a week later I sat with a family member while they received a life-changing diagnosis, and soon after that I finally ended a relationship that was no good for me. Looking back, it was clear that the universe was trying to tell me something. To be clear, all the manifestation practices in the world wouldn't have stopped those events from happening, but they might have limited the compounding emotional fallout that spilled over into other columns of my life. Friendships fell apart. Communication with my loved ones became non-existent, and the only things that seemed to take the edge off were drugs and alcohol. Late one late evening, nursing a large hangover, I decided to peruse the bookshelf of a family member and came across a book that was brilliant at explaining the basics of manifesting.

For a few weeks I was obsessed with my newfound powers. I used the power of positive thinking whilst I went to visit my father in the chapel of rest, and as I struggled to come to terms with the fact that I was light years behind my peers, who were all in stable relationships and even more secure jobs. But whilst my early experiments with manifesting helped take the edge off my grief, I was too young to understand how committed and intentional I needed to be to truly reap the rewards. Heck, I was still going to bed with my make-up on. There was no way in hell that I had the desire to start my day with a Gratitude Greeting (more on that later). Instead, the darkness of my life at the time was too all-consuming. I watched helplessly as fear's midnight-coloured cloak quickly consumed what little light manifestation had brought into my life.

Fast forward eight years and the powers of manifestation came knocking again. In less than a decade, so much had changed. This time I was twenty-nine, pregnant with my second child and living outside London, the city that had raised me. I was trying my best to break down the invisible but powerful wall that had positioned itself between the life I currently lived and the one I was beginning to understand that I deserved, but I felt ... stuck. My career felt unstable, personal debt hung like a noose around my neck and, having had a near-death experience giving birth to my daughter

Esmé, I was crippled by a fear of childbirth that was limiting my excitement about meeting my son.

Sporadically I would catch a whiff of how vibrant and expansive life could be, but as quickly as it came, it seemed to disappear. I wanted to feel positive about life, indefinitely not intermittently. In the background, I could hear the call to manifestation's magic growing ever louder. And I was desperate. So I dived down the manifestation rabbit hole, and I haven't come up since.

This time, I cut up the cloak of fear and decided to go all-in on designing the kind of life I wanted to live. Of course, this wasn't without difficulty, because by this point I was trying to undo three decades of listening to a negative soundtrack that was primarily sung by myself:

You're not worthy.

You don't have what it takes.

You don't deserve that.

I knew finding new tracks to play wasn't going to be easy, but I didn't expect the early days of my manifestation journey to be so exhausting. It is said that the average person has about sixty thousand thoughts per day. SIXTY THOUSAND. The material I engaged with in the early days of my journey made it clear that what I thought was everything. Being conscious enough to filter every thought is an impossible task. As the years went on, I would figure out a better hack for this (it's always about the feeling – more on that later) but in the early days, it was like playing tennis with a robot version of myself that would never tire of batting me a negative ball.

The truth is, if you've spent thirty years believing your negative thoughts and telling yourself negative things while also trying to flourish in environments that are trying to squish you, the initial turnaround is going to be so difficult that at times you're going to wonder if what you're trying to manifest – *this something that hasn't even materialised yet* – is, in fact, worth the hassle.

It always is.

I have spent the last seven years deeply working on unlocking the life I deserve. And with the thousands of hours I've dedicated to this task, one truth has become obvious to me. There's something that all these leaders, writers and educators teaching us how to manifest and be our 'best selves' have in common: they had a head start.

Let me explain.

The root of manifesting anything is *feeling*. Everything we manifest is born of thought and all thoughts are nurtured by how we feel. To be clear, this doesn't mean I agree with the idea that our thoughts are solely responsible for what happens to us. Not only is this a lazy concept, it is also harmful. A plethora of external factors including, but not limited to, structures, situations and our ranking in society are set in place around our experiences before anything happens in our lives. But once I understood how powerful feeling good was as a magnet for better, I had to acknowledge that I was attracting more of the same shit by allowing negativity to take up so much space in my head and heart.

The truth is, if you are lucky enough to be born in a physical form that begets the world's love, respect and attention, then there is a high likelihood that, more often than not, you are going to be feeling just fine. Why wouldn't you?

Society has always let you know that it 'has your back'.

The world has always let you know that you will be believed.

The world has always let you know that the body you exist in is worthy of care and respect.

The world has always shown you that it will find a way to support your every endeavour.

Traditional media has centred you, whether that's casting you as the lead in a soap opera or making sure someone like you is on the front cover of a magazine.

Social media has always offered you a fairer algorithm, allowing you to grow a platform that those who don't look like you will have to work tirelessly to achieve.

As consumer, you have seen positive reflections of yourself with every swipe.

Everything says: you belong here.

And what you believe about the world changes the way you behave.

And don't go thinking that all I'm talking about is white privilege. To convince you of that, I will use my very Black, very Nigerian husband Bodé as an example.

When we first started dating, I couldn't understand how blatant racial microaggressions seemingly went over his head like a rainbow. How could he be so confident in a society that would always find a way to blame him?

This all peaked one day when we were driving down a busy main road that gave way onto a dual carriageway. On the very narrow pavement was a little white girl, no more than two years old, gleefully using her little legs to move a pedal-less trike down towards the roundabout and into oncoming traffic.

Very quickly, we assessed that no other car was going to stop and help find out who this child's guardian was. My husband immediately pulled over and instinctively opened his door to get out.

'Where do you think you're going?' I snapped, eyes wide with horror.

He looked at me, confused.

'*I'm* going,' I yelled, 'The last thing I need is them pinning you as the big Black man who tried to kidnap a white toddler,' I growled, before hopping out of the car and sprinting towards the child.

Minutes later, after returning the little girl, who had gotten away from her heavily pregnant and now very emotional and thankful mother, I re-entered the car with a sense of heroism that was swiftly pierced by the sharpness of my husband's attitude.

'You didn't have to say it like that,' he sulked.

I felt five years' worth of annoyance rise to the surface.

'Listen, Imma need you to snap the fuck out of it, K?'

My south London razz was now on full display.

'This whole untouchable vibe you've got going on drives me crazy. You always assume the universe is going to have your back. News-flash, baby, this isn't Nigeria. You don't run tings here. In fact, in this country your Blackness doesn't keep you safe, it makes you a threat. That's what I've been trying not to say,' I spat, my chest heaving with a readiness to argue.

We sat in silence for the rest of the journey.

As the weeks went on, we were able to talk calmly about what had transpired.

'You're right, you know,' remarked Bodé, 'I never really noticed how being born into a society that always made it clear that I was going to be encouraged, believed and supported had a positive effect on me.'

'Mmm hmm,' I responded. 'I can't lie, more time I'm jealous of you,' I finally admitted.

He screwed up his face in a way that always makes me wonder whether I want to slap him or have sex with him. 'What, why?' he questioned.

'It's so hard to be born into a space that does the opposite. As a Black British woman, I would kill for some of the self-assuredness I see you possess. Goals that have felt almost impossible to attain would have been so much easier to achieve with that kind of attitude. You have no reason to believe that the space you inhabit is putting hurdles in your way. Little do you know that's more than half the battle behind you. You think you are worthy of having it all. And no one ever told you "No," or that you couldn't. You always saw yourself in all spaces and positions. So, whether you've realised it or not, your subconscious has agreed that you are in fact the shit, the numero uno, the don dadda. When it comes to manifesting, you have a brilliant head start.'

He nodded in wide-eyed agreement.

And that's how I came to understand that there are levels to this manifesting shit. It's all well and good to rattle on about the universe having your back when you're already a living example that it does. When you're born into a culture that welcomes you.

8

But what does manifesting look like if you're not:

white
thin
traditionally pretty
well-to-do
able-bodied
supported by nepotism
. . . or English isn't your first language?

What does manifesting look like if you see police killing your likeness whilst you struggle to communicate that you can't breathe?

What does manifesting look like if you have the talent but not *the look*?

What does manifesting look like if, for whatever reason, you exist on the periphery of society, you struggle with addiction, or you've been abused?

What does manifesting look like if you're a Black woman?

Well, see, that last question, I'm living it.

REJECT LOGIC AND EMBRACE MAGIC

The difference between the Candice of 2013 and the Candice of 2024 makes no logical sense. In 2013 I was by and a large a glass-half-empty type gal. Candice back then felt her goals were so out of reach, she didn't dare mention them out loud. Crushed by financial debt, she was positive about one thing: home ownership would never happen. And the relationship she was in? She knew it wouldn't last too long, so instead of waiting for its inevitable end, she took every opportunity she could to poke holes in it.

Just over a decade later, it's hard to believe that version of me even existed. Candice of 2024 has learned that it's best to make the dream a little bigger – it needs to make me nervous – because it will always be actualised. Not only is this Candice out of debt, she has savings and a will. She bought her first home in 2019, sold it to upgrade in 2021 and is even currently planning to buy an investment property. And that relationship? Well, twelve years in, it's a garden of love that continues to bloom.

2024 Candice has achieved things that many logical folk would say should take a lifetime. But one thing you will quickly realise if you want to make manifestation work for you, is that you better leave logic on the doorstep. She don't pay no rent here, sweetie.

The one thing I will continuously ask of you as you read this book is to **remain unrealistic**. Because when you're truly doing this practice correctly, the things and experiences you will be able to manifest will not be able to be explained logically. The quickest way to rob yourself of your innate power is to demand that life be 'realistic'.

To those who have been privy to what can only be described as my magical trajectory, one of the biggest questions I've been asked is how I've made life work in my favour. Whilst many would perhaps not want to share the how behind the change, this one I don't want to gate-keep. I have really struggled to find women who look like me who will share not only their journey with manifestation but also, most importantly, the positive results.

My Nigerian husband, who is from the Yoruba tribe, will often say *'Ti isu eni ba ta, afo wo bo je'* a proverb which loosely translates to 'if your yam is ready, you cover it and eat' but really means 'when you are blessed, you don't display it to the world.' And listen, I get it. Most of the Black community are warned against sharing the good elements of their life for fear of 'evil eye' or the idea that the jealousy of others may ruin their good thing. But I figure if we only get to see one kind of person enjoy their success or good fortune, how do we know it's possible for us?

I can't lie; in the early days of manifesting, I was just so geeked to learn about how I could better my life that I wasn't concerned who the messenger was. But I've come to find that the messenger does matter.

The reality is that if manifesting is something you want to explore, and if you aren't white and thin and pretty and able-bodied, there are a few more hurdles to overcome.

But fuck it, ain't we used to that by now?

So, what I hope this book does is allow you to learn about working with Source, the law of attraction and most importantly how to get into the flow of energy needed to manifest, whilst also leaving room for the fact that many of us trying to manifest are doing so in bodies that are very rarely loved, let alone protected.

Before we go any further, I want to bring clarity around the words and phrases that surround manifestation. You will find all of the following show up multiple times in this book, and often times I will use them interchangeably. These concepts are the foundations of manifesting and if, like me, you went to Sunday School and are familiar with the idea of the house built on sand, then I won't have to impress upon you how important it is to get your foundations as strong as they can be. The better the foundations, the easier the flow, the easier the flow, the quicker you arrive at your desired destination.

WHAT IS SOURCE?

Source, also referred to as source energy, is where all energy ends and begins. It is the starting point of all creation. Hindu philosophy will refer to this as 'Prana' which in Sanskrit translates to 'life force'. In Chinese philosophy this is referred to as Chi. And in West Africa it will often be called 'Nyama'. I add this to give examples of how universal the belief in Source actually is. Source energy can be found in every living thing, and is energy communicated as a **vibration.** As you deepen practices related to manifestation, you will often be able to feel the energy run through you like a soft hum. Without source energy there would be no manifesting, as there would be no energy to manipulate.

WHAT IS A VIBRATION?

A vibration is the energy communicated through a feeling. Most things like experiences, objects and even people can be classified as being of a 'high vibration' while others can be classified as a 'low vibration'. For example, spending time gossiping about others can for sure be categorised as a low vibrational activity. In contrast, spending that time going for a thirty-minute walk is unquestionably a high vibrational activity. We can also sense the vibrations of others or a scenario. That tingly feeling we get when our intuition tells us to move or go another way is us picking up on a low vibration. Us being drawn to people and things that make us feel good is because they omit a high vibration.

WHAT IS THE LAW OF ATTRACTION?

Think of the law of attraction (LOA) as your personal magnet. The law of attraction is simply believing that the energy you put out into the universe is the same energy you are going to call in. For those who believe, it is defined as a law, because there is simply no way around it. You cannot trick this magnet. Whatever it pulls in is based on the energy that was put out.

WHAT IS BEING 'IN FLOW'?

To be in flow means to trust in source energy. If at any point you are trying to manifest a thing or an experience and it feels as if there are too many obstacles in the way, or you don't one hundred per cent trust that your desires will come to fruition, you are not in flow. To be in flow is one of the most beautiful feelings as it is as natural as breathing. The goal is to remain in flow for as long as possible. There are many tips and tricks in this book that will help you get back to feeling in flow in no time at all.

SO WHAT IS MANIFESTING?

Manifesting is using source energy, the law of attraction and being in flow to help take your desires from dream space to real space. Manifesting is the outcome of learning and working with all of the above.

AND *MANIFEST(O)?*

The dictionary describes a manifesto as a 'written statement, that publicly declares the intentions, motives and views of its user'. So with that said, I want you to get to the end of this book and believe in your capability to design your own life, so much so that you are as enthused to share the results as if it were your personal manifesto. I hope *Manifest(o)* helps you to harness source energy and use the law of attraction to pull in more of what you do want, and gives you hacks to help you to stay in flow. It would mean everything to me if you found this book helpful enough that you felt confident enough to publicly declare how manifesting changed your life.

WHERE DO I START?

When it comes to starting manifestation the example I like to give is that it's quite like being given a blank sheet of paper in an art class as a child. In fact, my advice would be to do the same thing for yourself now – get hold of or just visualise a big piece of blank paper. But unlike in an art class, where you might be told to paint the same plant pot or cup of water as thirty other children, with manifestation you have complete creative control.

It's important that you see manifestation as the creative exercise that it is. If you approach manifestation with the same attitude you did, say, algebra (or anything else you thought you weren't good at) then you're going to find this process laborious. And as I've said before, no good thing can be manifested if logic is your starting block. It's time for you to release your inner magic.

Your blank page is your life itself in the most basic form. This white space represents the fact you are alive and, hopefully, well. The paintbrush and colours you will use represent your thoughts

15

and intentions, tools to be used however you wish. No one is stood before you dictating what or how you paint, so with that said, ask yourself: what do you want your life to look and feel like?

This is the difficult part. Even though we aren't given a specific still-life object to copy, most of us, by way of societal expectations, do already have a preconceived notion of what we believe a 'good' or 'successful' life looks like. As you work your way through this book, you will be encouraged multiple times to put whatever it is you've been told, or however you think you should be, into the margins. Manifestation is all about being in alignment with your deepest desires, not with the career counsellor who told you in Year Ten that you should get your head out of the clouds and be more realistic.

If your head is in the clouds, good – that where I need it to be. And if yours isn't there yet, no worries, this book is a first-class flight to getting there.

Unlike a child in art class, there are no time constraints as to how long painting this picture takes. To be real, as your masterpiece unfolds, it should take you the entirety of your life. Not because that's how long it takes to manifest – rather the complete opposite. Once you get in the groove and find yourself in flow, your desires will manifest so quickly that you will start to open up to the idea that this is how life feels now that you trust in your own power to create it.

When we begin to manifest, out of apprehension we typically start small. Not only is that fine, but it's also necessary, because there are levels. Expecting to get there all at once is like getting your first entry level job and expecting to be CEO by the end of the year.

Whilst yes, I reiterate that realistic isn't something you should be thinking about when you are manifesting, there is a process that you need to commit to without trying to skip steps. Why? Because at every level you are going to meet people and scenarios that are going to help you peel away another layer of the world's bullshit and help you understand not only what your deepest desires are, but most importantly the intentions behind them. Source loves a clear intention.

When I first started manifesting, I truly thought I wanted to be a Billionaire. Not a millionaire with a lower case 'm', but a Billionaire with a capital 'B'. I grew up with so little that I thought my deepest desire was to have more money than anyone could ever actually need. Now, although I am nowhere near Billionaire status, I can unequivocally proclaim that becoming one is *not* among my deepest desires. I understand now that that perceived desire grew out of a real one: to never have to worry about finances. As a Black woman from a working-class background, my desire is to have enough abundance in my life to politely decline an offer, because I no longer need to do something solely for money. But when I started manifesting, being a young Black girl from little to no means, I didn't have the experience, let alone the language, I needed to communicate my deepest desires to Source. So guess what Source did? It provided me with the access to people and scenarios that helped me scratch away at my belief, and figure out if my intention (to be financially supported enough to have a voice) was in alignment with my perceived desire (to be a Billionaire).

I've now shaken enough billionaires' hands to know that this specific monetary figure, a billion pounds, isn't my deepest desire. My deepest desire is to feel stable, provide a financial springboard for generations to come and, most importantly, be able to stand ten toes down on my 'no', and not worry that the next mortgage payment won't be met. You don't need to be a billionaire (with a big or small B) to do that. More to the point, the other things that are my deepest desires aren't in alignment with that. This isn't to say that no billionaire has a peaceful life, but having peeked behind the veil of such wealth, I can confirm that having that amount of cash does come with a few headaches. And as far as I'm concerned, you can't put a price on peace.

So as you start to toy with the tools that will help you develop your manifestation skills, you should prepare for a lot of redirection, because whatever you thought would be that life-changing thing may change shape right before your very eyes, as you are led closer and closer to the desires that are going to help you live consistently in flow. Also, the process of working out what our deepest desires are also gives us the space and time to get crystal clear about our intentions.

In the beginning my desire to be a Billionaire was also definitely rooted in the intention to be defined as an unequivocal success according to the world's standards. It was an intention rooted in ego more than anything. If I had done that work with the intention of wanting to accumulate that level of wealth so that I could be the world's largest philanthropist, it would have made for a different conversation entirely. The reason why I harp on about the importance of our intention is because intention is essentially the music and candles to manifestation's romantic date night. Get those things wrong and the vibes will be well off.

In the beginning you will find it easier to manifest physical things. So, this is what I am going to encourage you to do first. Because admittedly, when you begin this journey, you are going to want proof of all your hard work and the easiest way to do that is to, first and foremost, call in physical things. Energetically there is no difference between manifesting a new mobile phone or a new home. But because you are a beginner, you are going to have to work through a lot before understanding that, so once you've gone through all the tools in this book your first focus of manifestation should be something reasonably sized and tangible. Once you've called that in and you begin to understand how much creative control you have over your life, there will be no stopping you.

In the beginning of your manifesting journey, I would also advise that you focus on one thing at a time. Reason being, you are going to have to be mindful of your thoughts and feelings so much in the first instance that this will be hard work. Please note, if you are doing this correctly – you should feel exhausted. There is a lot of mental clearing-up to do to be in the optimum mode to manifest our dreams. I want you to understand that you can have all you want, whenever you want. It's like having constant access to a dessert buffet. There is no need to overstuff yourself on the first walk around – it will all still be there when you decide to circle back. So, start slow and have patience with yourself.

I also want you to understand that right now, your environment for manifesting is very important. When sitting down to use any of the tools in this book, the first few times you must endeavour to do so in a quiet, clutter-free space. Reason being, I am going to need you to limit any distractions and really centre yourself. Trying to connect with your deepest desires whilst also blocking out the *Peppa Pig* soundtrack is just not a vibe, OK?

Alongside this, I'm going to need you to get comfortable putting pen to paper. As I've matured in my manifestation journey, I am now able to manifest mentally. But in the early days of my practice, everything had to either be written down, or if I was using a vision board or three (see pages 67–76) I had to clap my eyes on them every day, multiple times a day. It is only through purposeful repetition that you are going to learn to override any negative narrative your brain has got used to telling you. As I said, as time goes on, you will be able to bring things into your reality simply by thought and feeling alone, but right now, you need to be dedicated to tangible routines that are going to help shift your mindset. Soon you will be so good at this, that you will start seeing **passive manifestation** come into play.

This happens to me a lot now. As an example, a few weeks ago, I was in a well known high-street store, mulling over the purchase of yet another brilliant pair of gold earrings. After a few moments' hesitation, I put the earrings back and thought:

'Cha, they will find me.'

Within a few days, a gift arrived for me. Within the packaging was not one but four pairs of new earrings, not just similar in style, but dare I say better than the ones I had been eyeing up a few days before.

This was the result of passive manifestation. I registered my interest, let it go and remained in good spirits. But I never consciously thought about it again. And just like that, better arrived at my doorstep.

The exciting thing about passive manifestation is that it's usually what leads to 'big magic'. When I refer to big magic, I'm talking about the moments of manifestation that are so mighty, no logical brain can explain them. They are just simple, undeniable magic. It's when a house that was previously off the market comes back on the week you start looking for your dream home, or when, on a random night out you bump into the person you always felt you were destined to be with, but lost contact with years ago. Yeah, those moments are the ones worth playing this game for.

With that said, it's time to begin.

PART 1

Your Manifestation Magic Toolbox

Before we start to tear at the meat of this manual, I would like to provide you with a skeleton, a framework, if you will, which I simply call my 'magic toolbox'. The practices in this magic toolbox – no matter what kind of manifestation you attach them to – have come to be the ones I return to time and time again.

I truly believe that each tool has its use, and all manifestations become infinitely more powerful when we deploy one or all of these tools in order to support and propel our deepest desires.

The tools are as follows:

ASKfirmations

Meditation

Gratitude

Scripting

Vision Boarding

Crystals and Cleansing

It's important for me to stress that these tools are such workhorses they could each easily have a book of their own. Unfortunately, we don't have an eternity together, so where possible please feel free to research deeper into the power of each tool on your own.

Let's unlock the box.

♀ ASKFIRMATIONS

Prior to picking up this book, if you had an even passing interest in manifestation chances are you'll have heard about affirmations. You know, you stand in front of the mirror and recite positive phrases about yourself such as:

I am so smart.

I am kind.

I am talented.

I am loved.

I am so *insert wish here*.

The universal thinking behind the classic affirmation practice is that if you say something positive about yourself enough times, you will one day believe it.

For some, affirmations are among the hardest working tools in their toolbox. But personally I have always struggled with them. And when I shared that with my close friends, they agreed that affirmations were their biggest hurdle too.

The trouble was, when I started affirmations, I found that my brain was always wired to counteract my claim. For example, I would say, 'I am so smart,' and force a smile to appear on my face, and reflection in the mirror.

Within seconds my brain would respond:

'Really? So how come you failed those GCSEs and you don't have a degree?'

Ouch.

I would persist:

'I am so kind.'

Boom, the takedown would be swift.

'That's funny; I'm sure we both overheard that ex-friend on the phone to her boyfriend that time, calling you a selfish bitch.'

One last time, I'd mutter to myself,

'I am so pretty.'

'OK, now you must want to be a comedian, 'cause you only need to hop online to be told how undesirable you are.'

I think you get my point. Especially in the early days of manifesting, it can feel more work than it's worth to try and override the super-strong negative discourse we have about ourselves. We live in a capitalist society devoted to selling us goods and services we don't really need. We are more valuable when we are down, or when we feel that we are lacking in some way because it's then that we might make a purchase sold to us as 'this is going to change it all'. I can't tell you how many fast fashion pieces I've purchased, certain that the package will land with some extra self-confidence thrown in. Meanwhile, most of us women have been raised to believe that saying anything nice about ourselves will be read as us being too self-absorbed or full of ourselves. Early on, we are taught to put positive self-talk on mute, because boasting isn't cute! Society has found that it's easier to manipulate us if we believe we ultimately have no control about how good, full and rich our lives can be.

I have found that our logical brains are hardwired to put up a fight, especially when we're trying to convince ourselves of positive realities that our subconscious knows we don't yet believe to be the actual truth. What typically happens when we affirm something positive about ourselves is that our logical brain swoops in, like a petulant toddler who's been told they have to wait their turn for the building blocks. They don't want to be patient, they just want to kick that shit over! Like I said, if you're waiting for your logical brain to be an instrument of magic making, then I regret to inform you: that particular wand is always going to be broken.

Don't let small logic erode big magic.

History has a part to play here too. If you've found manifestation in the second, third or fourth quarter of your life, I have to tell you time has not been on your side. Welcome to what is for sure the beginning of the best part of your life, but remember you have at the very least two decades of negative programming that now need a hard and fast factory reset. Which is why, when it comes to building the life of my dreams, I'll take any available shortcut to thinking better.

So I would like to share a hack I have learned that has quickly replaced affirmations for me. It is the ASKfirmation. Oh, you're going to want to pull up a chair for this one.

The ASKfirmation isn't entirely different from the affirmation. In both cases you are trying to affirm something that you may not yet one hundred per cent believe. But the difference, and therefore the change, lies in turning the affirmation into a question.

Why am I so loved?

Why am I so healthy?

Why am I so abundant?

Why am I so supported?

The first time I replaced affirmations with ASKfirmations, I was blown away. Immediately, instead of searching for ways to sabotage the new way I was trying to speak (and therefore think) about myself, my logical brain just busied itself with searching for answers.

You are so loved because you are worthy of being loved.

You are healthy because you are learning to make better choices for your mind and body.

You are so abundant because you understand that, like the vastness of the ocean, there is nothing lacking.

You are supported because you are surrounded by people who love to see you flourish.

On and on it went because, instead of being one and done, my mind went on a marathon hunt for multiple ways it could answer my questions, and examples it could mentally attach to those answers to support them.

Now, with a little more manifesting magic under my belt, I

understand that the reason I struggled with affirmations was because the intention of those statements was to fundamentally overwrite my negative thought patterns. Maybe one day my subconscious would have finally got itself together and come to my defence, but I had to recognise that using affirmations in this way was going to take an amount of time that I didn't necessarily have.

A conversation with my daughter Esmé, who was then nine years old, made it very clear to me just how early our logical brain starts to try and be the loudest in the room.

'Yeah, I just don't get it, when Rebecca says I have a good running stride, immediately a voice in my head goes, so why aren't you a faster runner then?' she admitted one day, looking at me through my vanity mirror as I sat doing my make-up.

I looked back at her in the mirror.

'That's because part of your brain is always trying to take you down a peg or two. What I want you to try and do in those situations is first, **catch it**.'

And that's also my first piece of advice for you, dear reader. You have to get into the habit of catching negative thoughts about yourself. There is no point in pretending that you are not struggling to see the best in yourself. Your subconscious has already registered it, so I beg you, drag that bitch kicking and screaming out into the light. Then take time to really scrutinise and interrogate not only what your initial thoughts and feelings were, but also where they came from.

'The second step is to **kill it**,' I told my daughter.

This can be done by knowing what makes you feel good about yourself. This is your most dependable murder weapon. For those of us new to this, it will often start by using attributes that others have praised us for as our first line of defence.

'My partner says I'm so helpful.'

'My friends say I'm very trustworthy.'

'My boss says I always go above and beyond.'

The issue with depending on compliments from other people is that they are often skewed towards the skills and attributes you have that a person knows work well for them, and not necessarily the things that make *you* most proud of you. It's important to identify this distinction so that we don't end up being addicted to whatever version of us works best for others.

'And then of course the final step is to **bin it**,' I told her. 'This can be done simply by asking your brain some positive questions about yourself.'

My daughter scrunched up her nose.

'Mum, catch it, kill it, bin it? Isn't that for, like, viruses?' she giggled.

'Exactly!' I exclaimed. 'Show me a more killer virus than thinking poorly about yourself.'

'OK, you've got points,' she shot back.

'More than. I don't know how many times I have to tell you this, but as a little Black girl, you are going to grow into a tremendously beautiful and intelligent Black woman, whom the world has been taught to fear. The world deals with that fear by shutting you down and making you feel as though you have no value. How you think and feel about yourself is going to make all the difference,' I finished, making sure we made eye contact.

'Uh huh,' she nodded.

By then I'd been parenting long enough to know two things: firstly, I didn't need a grand expression to confirm that something had indeed resonated with her; secondly, our actions always, always, speak louder than words. So, the very next day, I decided to begin seeding the power of ASKfirmations by being the one to pose the positive questions.

'Esmé, why are you so talented?' I asked her over breakfast.

She paused and then shrugged, 'I dunno . . .' she began.

I cut her off sharply.

'Aht aht aht – remember what we were saying yesterday?' I waited and watched as she mentally began to open her brain's curtains.

'Oh, yeah.'

'Right, so let's try that again. Esmé, why are you so beautiful?'

'Um, because you're my mum.'

'Ooo nice, wasn't expecting that, but thank you. Let's try one more time. Esmé, why are you so beautiful?'

'I just am. It's true,' she laughed.

Since then, I have made it a habit to implement ASKfirmations not only with my family, but also with my friends. At first it was funny to watch people be confused about how to respond to questions about themselves in a positive manner. But after a week or so, perhaps through new habits or even annoyance, everyone was getting on board. It was so refreshing to hear everyone in my closest network say positive things about themselves. And Esmé? Well, her most recent school report said that one area she doesn't struggle with is her confidence. I know for sure working with ASKfirmations has had a positive impact in that regard.

Please note an ASKfirmation is not the same thing as giving a compliment. I have found that, much like affirmations, when it comes to compliments it seems our logical brain's first line of defence is instantly to get to work trying to catch, kill and bin any kind words which are thrown our way.

For example, a co-worker might say, 'Oh, I love your outfit today. You look so good.'

And instead of allowing ourselves to be in agreement with the 'good', we go racing to catch the bad: 'Urgh this old thing! It's all that was clean. Plus, I haven't been to the gym in ages.'

Even for those who have mastered the art of catch it, kill it, bin it, compliments can be the one arena in which they still feel nervous. Instead, ASKfirmations simply allow us the room to tend to our own garden of positivity.

The beautiful thing about ASKfirmations is this can very quickly become a community exercise. (As we'll discuss in the 'Happiness' section of this book, another way to put the magic of our life on super steroids is to harness the collective positive energy of others.) You can turn this into a game between family, friends, lovers and co-workers. Like I said, at first expect some resistance across the board as there are so few of us who are in the habit of thinking well about ourselves, let alone asking ourselves why we are so badass every chance we get.

I find ASKfirmations to be especially brilliant when I am lacking in confidence. As you read this book, you'll see I've tried to pepper in real-life examples as often as possible. Today provided me with the perfect opportunity to do so.

I am writing this on a plane to New York City, cruising at an altitude of 12,080 metres and a speed of 740 kilometres per hour. Whilst I've perhaps made it no secret that one of my life goals is to relocate myself and my family to a stunning Brooklyn brownstone (seriously, it's currently the screensaver on my phone), I have accepted that the path towards getting there must unfold in a way that I have little say over. Because I'll be transparent: Do I currently have the five million dollars plus that the Zillow app tells me I need to acquire my dream home? Absolutely not. Am I letting my current reality stop me from believing that there are multiple pathways that could open up in order to make that home mine? Also, absolutely not.

Logic doesn't belong here.

Learning that I don't get to have a say in how a desire materialises has been the hardest part of manifesting to get my head around. The reason why we don't get a say in 'how' it comes to be is because our logical brains are perhaps only going to provide us with five different winning routes. Whereas the Source has access to *millions*. Us thinking we know best can get us in a right pickle, and create unnecessary resistance. And you know what?

Manifestation hates resistance.

To resist is to lose before your toe has even touched the start line.

If you want to be waiting forever and a day for your desires to become your reality, waste your energy trying to control how it comes to pass. You will leave yourself bent out of shape and exhausted. To submit is to show true courage, and trust in the fact that the universe always, always delivers.

As with all my manifestations, my sole purpose in manifesting my move to NYC was to focus on what I could manage, what I could commit to. And that would be to catch, kill and bin negative thoughts. Engage in acts and spend time with people that made me feel good and most importantly work hard to live life as if it had all already come to pass.

I had to think of ways to get that tingly feeling New York gives me as much as possible. Because doing so would ensure that I was in flow. Slowly, I began to sow the seed.

'I think it will be helpful if I try to get to the city at least once a quarter. You know, just to network and start establishing some work connections,' I said flippantly to my husband six months ago, after musing over the fact that the glass ceiling of my current existence felt as though it was about to collapse on me.

'I hear that. You know I'll follow you wherever you go; we just have to pattern it well for the kids,' said Bodé, 'You do your thing with the magic and when you need me, I'll run the numbers for the logic,' he finished, describing our tendencies perfectly.

So that's what I did. I got comfortable in the knowledge that once I had made the desires of my heart crystal clear, I had to trust that a) my order had been placed and b) my desire would be delivered. Like many, I have desires that, off the rip, don't seem easy to bring to fruition. Like: there is no connect, no great aunt who is going to leave me a brownstone in her will. To be honest, these are my favourite kind of manifestations – the ones that are seemingly impossible.

So, over the course of the past six months, I've intermittently been using all the tools in my magic toolbox to start bringing this manifestation into my current reality, including ASKfirmations.

'Candice, why does Brooklyn look so good on you?' I ask myself. **'Why have the kids settled in and found their tribe so quickly?'** **'How has this move enabled your husband to see how many ways his talents can be used for good?'**

The wonderful thing is, ASKfirmations can be modified for any situation. So yes, whilst we haven't physically made that leap yet, we can get in flow faster by using ASKfirmations to get our brains excited for our upcoming reality.

Right, let's get back on track. Why the hell am I spilling all of this while this plane hurtles towards the place my heart wants to call home? Because to most, it might seem like the invitation I accepted, the reason for my flight, came like a bolt out of the blue.

Two months prior to me boarding this flight, it was past bedtime when I heard the familiar ping that alerted me to a new email. It was from my then-manager. I toyed with leaving it until the morning, but I was not quite ready to sleep yet. So, I snatched my phone off the stand, in no way prepared for what I was about to read.

With every line my eyes scanned, I sat up more and more, trying not disturb my Prince Charming getting his beauty sleep.

'Jesus, this is HUGE,' I said.

'Rah,' I exhaled to myself, as I finished the email, signed off by Bill and Melinda, founders of the Gates Foundation.

They were inviting me to be part of their social cohort for the Foundation's annual awards and conversation, Goalkeepers 2023. Both events would take place in New York City. The foundation would sort and cover everything and most importantly pay me for the pleasure of my company, as this year's conference was about a conversation dear to my heart – the subject of my first book, *I Am Not Your Baby Mother* and perhaps how you came to engage with my work in the first place – Black maternal health. The fact that the events were not only taking place in the city of my dreams, but were also rooted in my most authentic work, was not lost on me.

Whilst a part of me wanted to jump on the bed and wake up the whole household – not necessarily because of who had invited me, but because I was watching big magic at work – instead I allowed myself to sink back under the duvet and simply whisper, 'Thank you.'

Because clearly, my order was being processed. And whilst I was never in doubt of it coming to pass, the how (which, remember, we should never concern ourselves with) was so far beyond anything I could have positioned for myself, all I could do was show gratitude for how the game was being rigged to work in my favour.

But what makes this example even sweeter is how, at every point, I've had to use ASKfirmations to remind myself of how worthy I am, of not just this, but anything at all.

Now, whilst this is of course a book you can read (or listen to), I want you to understand this is a book you must also **do**. The **doing** is a major part of the manifestation process. I can *wish* to live in a gorgeous Brooklyn brownstone all I want. But if I'm not making choices that can inspire physical action towards getting there, no matter how infinitesimal they seem, then I should just forget about it. These practices are all about developing habits. It is only through habit that we are going to be able to turn the volume down on the negativity or pushback we feed ourselves until eventually they're on mute entirely. And that's where ASKfirmations come in.

So now I would like to invite you to try ASKfirmations for yourself. As a loose rule, I encourage beginners to frame their ASK-firmations around who they really want to **be**, not necessarily what they would like to **have**. Reason being, is because how we feel about ourselves will have a direct correlation to how easily we can attract what we would like to own. You cannot send out vibrations of self-hate and then expect a new house or designer handbag at the end of it. It all starts with you. And the very few who are able to acquire a desire without mastering their self-talk always seem to lose it all and end up back at square one. And I wouldn't want that for you.

So, no skipping steps. Because if you choose to do that, you are choosing to ignore the energetic roadblocks between the life you currently live and the one you desire.

Unlike traditional affirmations, a mirror is not necessary, unless you would like to do it that way. However, I would suggest that for the first few times, you may want to write your ASKfirmation down using a pen and paper as you may find you're not able to answer the question immediately or succinctly. Writing it down leaves physical space for you to return to it another time.

Now, the question for your ASKfirmation is up to you, but remember, like I said, beginners should focus on questions relating to who they are and how they show up in the world, not questions tied to material possessions.

For instance, as I write this, I'm currently at a crossroads in my career. I would like to grow my platforms in the space of healing, self-help and community by way of public speaking, podcasts and real-life tours. But the gag is, the idea of keynote speeches knocks the wind out of me. I cannot tell you how many times my speaking agent has told me that not feeling confident about myself in this area is holding me back. Time and time again I've turned down the opportunity to deliver a keynote speech to a powerful audience that I knew could help position me in a whole new light. I know this is an energetic block between who I am now, and the person I desire to be.

So my question would be:

'Why am I such an accomplished public speaker?'

Admittedly, this is the first time I've done this particular ASK fir-mation so you are watching me work through this in real time.

Why am I such an accomplished public speaker?

I am such an accomplished speaker because the message I am destined to share is bigger than the fear.

'Why am I such an accomplished public speaker?'

I am an accomplished public speaker because I've spent time practising my keynote speech.

'Why am I such an accomplished public speaker?'

I am an accomplished speaker because I have worked with sup-portive people who understand what it takes to create an engaging keynote speech.

I wish you could sit with me now to feel this immediate energy shift – it feels electric. My entire being is already flooding with a more positive vibration and although I'm still nervous, I feel more confident in the brilliant public speaker I am destined to be.

I will continue to focus on this specific ASKfirmation over the next week. Where possible I will do this as a written exercise as this is a new ASK for me, and I want to get my brain into the habit of speaking well about myself in this area.

Of course, there will be many things you will want to ask of yourself, but I always advise to take it as slow as possible. Try not to juggle more than three ASKfirmations at any one time. As you grow more confident in your brain's natural desire to give you positive feedback, you will find that you are able to use ASKfirmations at any time, using the privacy of internal dialogue. I have found a silent ASKfirmation can flood my system with positive feelings, time and time again.

MEDITATION

Like many people, I came to meditation kicking and screaming.

Shortly after the chaotic and near-death event that was the birth of my daughter Esmé, I just couldn't settle my mind. Days and, most annoyingly, nights were spent overthinking, with the noise of the world – literally and figuratively - only getting louder and louder. Post-partum depression (see pages 200–2) and prolonged grief disorder, piled on top of the day-to-day drudgery of just getting by, left me feeling as though I was all at once fit to burst and unable to breathe.

I cannot now recall whether it was a video, book or podcast that informed this decision, but one day, I decided to just try and meditate. With no guidance, I sat cross-legged on my bedroom floor, closed my eyes and just decided to breathe. Once my vision was limited, my hearing immediately grew sharper, and the noise of the busy main road close to our tiny flat proceeded to grow like an orchestra made up of bus engines, honking horns and yelling teenagers.

I tried to take more deep breaths.

Was that something crawling on me? I let one eyelid fly open. No, nothing.

Sighing, I closed my eyes again.

More deep breaths.

Now the shrill stabbing sound of our flat buzzer went.

'For fuck's sake!' I yelled, lurching into a yoga pose similar to Cat-Cow before rolling off the bed.

I yanked the receiver off the wall.

'Hi, package for number 11,' spat a gruff voice.

'Wrong num–'

'Yeah I know that, love but can I jus–'

I pressed the entry key before heading back to the bed. Looking at the time, I clocked I only had ten minutes before I had to collect Esmé. Nothing about this process felt calm or relaxing.

It didn't matter anyway because I had already decided meditation wasn't for someone like me. Working-class Black women didn't have time for all that 'self-care' malarkey. That was for those rich enough to live in India for a year – you know, the ones who wear the massive harem pants and decide being vegan is personality trait. Yeah, mediation was for them and monks. I was neither, I reminded myself.

I shoved down the desire to get to grips with this practice that a higher me knew I so desperately needed.

'You have to return to this,' a whisper said to me.

'Later,' I said aloud.

A few months passed before I felt the pull again.

'You need to learn how to meditate,' the whisper urged.

Looking back, what that whisper knew was that to try to manifest without understanding the importance of meditation is like learning to drive without understanding the importance of your Highway Code. As my taste for manifestation grew, I needed to get to grips with developing the habit of listening to myself.

By now, I had done a little more research, and I understood that guided meditation was perhaps the best approach for a novice like me. I searched up the best apps for this sort of thing and I stumbled across one called Headspace.

The flat was once again empty. I opened the app and simply searched for something for beginners. Determined to stay focused, I came armed with headphones this time, a big over-the-head pair which I was sure would block out the world of sounds around me.

I opted for the shortest session and just listened to the narrator Andy's voice.

Sure, there were a few moments when I felt as if I would burst into flames, but before I knew it the five minutes were up.

I've got to keep it real. I felt so . . . underwhelmed.

Was that it?

Where was my moment of calm? My spiritual Big Bang? My time with the big woman upstairs?

Aside from feeling relatively weightless for perhaps thirty seconds, nothing major happened – but it didn't stop me from trying the next day. And the day after that. And the day after that.

Soon I came to understand that there is no arrival point in meditation, there is simply *being*.

And because we are human, sometimes just 'being' is difficult.

Over the past six years, I can count on the fingers of one hand the number of times I've meditated and felt as though I fully transcended. Like I rose up out of my body and could have a good old gander at what was before and what was to come. And whilst those very rare experiences are like a warm hug I could relax into for an eternity, they happen too sporadically to be the reason that I return to meditation, time and time again.

I return to meditation just to be.

In a hyper-connected world, which will fight for our attention from the second we wake to the moment we (struggle to) fall asleep, meditation is the only time I can fully be present and spend uninterrupted time with myself.

I have been extra-dependent upon meditation during times of high anxiety, confusion and helplessness. I see meditation like finally listening to your laptop's cry for you sort through the storage. When my mind goes into overdrive, surrendering to a moment of meditation is how I drag unnecessary files into the trash and free up some storage in my headspace for the things that make me feel better. Even when I go into a meditation session with no conscious questions, it is usually through meditation – that moment of quiet – that I will hear the subconscious answer to a question I've clearly been harbouring all along. Connecting with my breath, internal and external energy has been a major key for me in being clear about what I would like to manifest.

I totally understand our innate fear of sitting with ourselves. Much like going to therapy, when you allow yourself that kind of space, you are undoubtedly going to, at times, be presented with a problem, a version of yourself or a question that you have been avoiding. And there is no one more avoidant than me.

I believe the reason we don't enjoy sitting with ourselves is because often a lie feels so much more soothing than the truth. The core of you, the subconscious that is always whirring away in the background – that version of you would know that, for example, you have long since given up on your marriage. But to allow that truth to expand is to face that there is often a lot of mess in between the version of you now (in this scenario, married but sad and low in self-esteem) and the version of you (happier, healthier, divorced) that you dream about. That can be too much to deal with.

Often the distance between who we are and who we want to be is longer and steeper than we imagined. And because we are OK here, as we currently are, it's often far easier to stay busy, connected and over-worked so that we don't have to recognise that 'OK' is simply that: the C-minus version of life, when what you really want is to get closer to that A-plus version of you.

Developing the habit of meditation is going to make you privy to all the desires you've allowed your current life to suck the colour out of. Meditation is going to help reveal the truth about your desires and how you are stopping yourself from getting there.

If you are new to all things manifesting then, like me, you might struggle to see yourself as someone who meditates. Perhaps you have never seen yourself represented in meditation. Or going deeper still, perhaps you have never deemed yourself worthy of that alone time. For some it's fear. The noise of the world is our greatest distraction. To allow all versions of yourself to meet, without ego, is a bold and brave choice to make – and at its core, that is what meditation is: sitting with the truest version of yourself.

'*OK, Candice. But what if I'm not ready for that yet?*' I hear you say.

Well then, I would like you to accept that irrespective of its use to manifesting, meditation, at the bare minimum, is good for both your mental and physical health. Although I love the opportunities that technology has provided, it must also be said that tech is also one of the biggest reasons many of us are struggling. Offer yourself some peace and respite by inviting meditation into your life as a form of self-care instead of looking at it as a way to get a new car. As you develop a personal relationship with meditation, you will come to understand how important it is but, in the meantime, be willing to trick yourself into spending time with yourself in this capacity simply because you deserve it.

Long before I began my manifesting journey, I got a tattoo that reads 'Meet me halfway'. It's actually a nod to my father, as that was his standard response whenever I asked him for something.

'Dad, can I have forty quid please?'

'Ah come on, Cand,' he would respond with a cheeky glint in his eye. 'You know you've got to . . .'

'. . . meet me halfway!' we would say in unison, with me rolling my eyes.

Of course, as I got older, I learnt to just double the figure before I started so that halfway was what I wanted. But what Dad taught me, and lived by his example, was that you have to be willing to bring something to the table.

Manifesting is the same: you must register your interest. You must be willing to step out of your comfort zone. You must gather the confidence to try something new.

Manifesting is always going to require you to make the first move.

There will be many times over in this book that I will remind you I'm not with the bullshit, OK? Manifesting isn't all glitter and rainbows. It's work. And we have to be willing to put the work in.

So, I'll be frank, deciding to try and learn to manifest without investing in meditating is just plain lazy. Because in my opinion, if you can't sit with the most stripped-back version of yourself, then how will you know what you – the realest version of you, not the one you present to the world in order to feel safe and accepted – really want? When you meditate, you make space to learn what your deepest desires are and when you know this, you can set intentions that are in alignment with your highest self.

Exactly.

OK, Candice, no need to shout, I heard you. So how, exactly, do I meditate?'

Well, now, I don't know if I'll be able to answer that.

Girl, stop playing with me.

No, in all seriousness – how to meditate is different for everyone. And it must be said that I do not see myself as a meditation teacher

(I find it incredible that there are in fact schools that offer to teach you how become one) so I won't be providing you with a guide on how to meditate.

But I do have some basic pointers to help you get started:

1. Because I'm not a teacher, I am always going to encourage the use of guided meditation. I've been practising for years, and I have never, ever done so without the use of an app or video to help guide me through my practice. (My particular favourite is the Headspace app, but many fitness apps now have meditation classes available that I've found to be just as good.) As with all things, there will of course be people who look down upon this and don't see it as 'true' meditation. To those people, I say that their version of meditation can't be working because anyone who meditates knows that judgement doesn't belong here.

2. Where possible, meditate in a space with few disturbances. If you live in a busy household, schedule your sessions for when your space has the least traffic. What time of day you choose depends on your desires. If you have a rushed, anxiety-inducing day ahead, I would recommend meditation as the way you start your day. If you struggle to sleep, it should be the way you end your day. I am flexible about the times I meditate and have often dipped into it multiple times a day.

3. If you are new to meditation (or if you're an oldie but you're tired) remember there is no required time goal to hit that will then allow you to call yourself a master meditator. I meditate for any

length of time between ten to thirty minutes; the former always flies by and the latter can often feel hellish, so my sweet spot is twenty minutes. But you can just start with one minute. Something is better than nothing.

4. Whilst most will say practice makes perfect, this isn't the case for meditation. In fact, in meditation there is no need for you to search for any progress at all. In the physical world, we have been taught to collect data so we can track progress, thereby developing the idea that less is bad and more is good. This is not the vibe around meditation. The only requirement is just to arrive and be. Just doing that makes you a winner.

5. No form of meditation trumps the other. Humans have ruined everything, including every string attached to the bow of self-care, by making us feel as though we aren't naturally 'good at' something so it can then be monetised and sold back to us as the answer. Meditating with a free guided meditation app or a free YouTube video is just as valid and rewarding as developing a relationship with transcendental meditation (TM) and then having the privilege to decide to live in an ashram for a year. Whether you prefer to be guided by the dulcet voice of a stranger or just to sit with your own breath is purely down to personal preference, but meditation isn't something that needs to be supported by capitalism. So no need to add anything to your Amazon basket in order to do this the 'right' way.

6. Speaking of personal preference, that goes for your desired pose too. For a long time, I thought sitting cross-legged with the

straightest back, palms turned outwards on knees was the only 'right' way to meditate. Turns out, I'm a Corpse Pose kind of gal. Don't get bent out of shape trying to follow others; allow your body to fold into the pose most suited for you.

7. It is important that you don't put pressure on meditation and what you assume it should do for you, or what it should feel like. Every time I meditate, I'm met with a different outcome. I have learned that even if a session doesn't feel like a victory, it is exactly what I need at the time.

8. Meditation is not about trying to quiet the mind. Whilst it is magical when this happens, when you first begin to meditate a silent mind is very rarely the experience. In the first few instances you will find it troublesome to quiet your mind as all manner of thoughts and worries are going to come flooding in. For those of you who are parents, the thoughts are similar to that moment you have just put your baby or toddler down for a nap, and in the quiet you can really assess how messy the place has become in the last few hours. For a while the silence will only highlight the mess. But unlike in life, meditation doesn't call for you to clean it up. If thoughts come into your head – no matter how trivial or important you deem them to be – acknowledge them, and then release them.

9. You must understand that, as with every piece of advice in this book, you are only going to see results with consistency. You cannot meditate once a month and then claim that it's doing nothing for you. At the bare minimum you are going to want to commit to ten minutes, three times a week. We all have that time

available to us. As I began to develop my practice I found myself yearning for it in times of stress and worry. It becomes a cheap and easy way for you to manage difficulties or find balance. Your body will naturally end up craving more.

10. Enjoy yourself! I approach every practice with joy and gratitude. Speaking of which . . .

GRATITUDE

As soon as my eyes open, before I reach for my phone or swing my feet out of the bed, I lie in silence, look up at the ceiling and think of five things I am grateful for. Gratitude is stronger than any coffee.

The things I am giving thanks for, at the root of it, are inconsequential. It's the thanking itself that kicks me into a high vibration. What gratitude does is help produce feelings of happiness and satisfaction. And, as I will continue to say throughout this book:

The first and most important step to manifesting is *feeling*.

Saying you're in good health is different to *feeling* as though you are.

Saying you are wealthy is different to *feeling* as if you are.

Saying you are happy is different to *feeling* that you are.

We can say anything we like, but our body responds to nothing as quickly or as strongly as feeling.

Most people allow the physical outside world to inform how they feel about themselves on the inside, instead of understanding that how we feel about ourselves on the inside is what shapes our experience of the physical world.

But if you want to change how you feel at lightning speed, you're going to need some hacks. And one of the biggest ways to hack how you're feeling and inspire a higher vibration is with gratitude. It really is the strongest tool in the box.

'But Candice, I don't feel as though I currently have anything to be grateful for.'

You always do.

'My health isn't where I would like it to be.'

You woke up this morning.

'Bills are piling up.'

You have the opportunity to brainstorm new ways to boost your income.

'I don't like my current accommodation.'

You aren't homeless.

'I am homeless.'

You woke up this morning.

I must remind you that I don't enjoy speaking from my arse, so when I say I have faced every 'negative' I've presented above, I really mean it. Even when it seems like there is nothing to be thankful for, you can strip it back and find something. When I wasn't yet living in the accommodation of my dreams, sometimes I could only find gratitude for the fact I had clean running water, but honestly, that would be enough to pull me through.

Each and every time I have deployed the tool of gratitude, there has been such a colossal energy shift that, even if it has taken my physical world some time to catch up, spiritually I immediately feel as if I can change my perspective on the situation, no matter how dire it may appear.

During the first lockdown in 2020, my then two-year-old son Richard (whom we call RJ) fell gravely ill. What began as the 'typical' childhood illness chickenpox ended up with him developing a flesh-eating bacterial infection, which made his face so swollen he was temporarily blinded. To add further strain, a day after my son was admitted to hospital, his father, my husband Bodé, announced that he too had fallen ill with chickenpox, for the first time in his life. Chickenpox in adult males can be deadly.

The idea that we would be able to care for our son in shifts (as during the pandemic only one caregiver was allowed into hospital at any given time) was immediately eradicated. I had to be not only our son's primary carer, but also to sort childcare for Esmé, who was seven years old at the time and, of course, try to ensure that my husband was cared for too.

After RJ's second night in hospital, it became clear that he wasn't getting any better. He was so dehydrated it was proving impossible to administer a drip to offer intravenous meds, which meant that every four hours, even if he was asleep, he had to be woken up to have injections directly into his muscles.

On the third morning, the doctor let me know the course of

action: 'If Richard is unable to turn a corner, we may need to induce a coma, just to make sure this swelling doesn't get out of hand.'

I had to reach out for the cold metal bedframe to stop the world from spinning. As his mother, I had known the situation was bad before having this discussion, but having to hear this alone, with no one else for moral support, was a blow I wasn't ready for. Ever so slightly the idea that I might potentially leave this hospital, the same hospital RJ had been born in two years ago, without him began to take hold.

Later that evening, after spoon-feeding him his paltry meal, I was lying in the semi-darkness trying to get comfortable on a cold and hard parent cot, when, through tears, I decided it was time to squint and see the good in all of this.

At least he has his own room.

And yes, this cot is hard, but I'm sure it's way more comfortable than a chair.

Thankfully the nurses help me watch him, so I can go and grab food.

I know Esmé is safe with her godmother.

And you know what, even if he doesn't pull through, this boy has given us a great two years.

Even though I was crying thinking these things, it really helped. Slowly but surely, metaphorical slices of sun started to cut through this dark and heavy cloud. To be clear, I had even decided to find gratitude in the worst possible outcome of this situation. I told myself:

Even if he dies, Candice, you've felt pain like this before. You will be able to support his dad and his sister.

Be grateful for the time you have alone with him now.

Then, as if I was following an invisible piece of string holding us together, I climbed into RJ's hospital bed and just cuddled with him until we were both awoken for his next injections. Perhaps it was the act of physically and, most importantly, mentally submitting to this situation, but I fell into the most peaceful sleep I had since the entire nightmare had begun. A little later I was awoken by a delighted nurse who whispered that finally RJ's temperature had begun to come down and, should that continue, there could perhaps be some light at the end of this tunnel.

By the time the sun came up, his temperature had fallen a little more, and for the first time in days, he asked to watch something on his iPad.

It felt like a miracle, made even more magical by the fact that when I called my husband, it sounded as if he too had turned a corner. It would be nearly another week and what felt like hundreds of tests later before RJ was discharged, but to be honest, I would have stayed in that hospital another year, as long as it meant I was able to leave with him alive and well.

I've since deleted all the images I had of RJ with a swollen head and clearly infected facial wounds. Some images are clear enough to exist in memory alone. But what I can never forget is the community that rallied around us at the time. I am so grateful to everyone who understood what I needed in that moment, even if I couldn't verbalise it for myself. And most of all I'm grateful for my knowledge of just how powerful being grateful can be.

Now, being grateful is one thing but *showing* gratitude can be the fast track to a higher vibration.

You can be grateful for your current car, but you *show* gratitude by keeping it clean.

You can be grateful for the clothes you currently own, but you *show* gratitude by following the care label, ironing out wrinkles and replacing missing buttons.

You can be grateful for your current job role, but you *show* gratitude by applying yourself, being on time and doing it to the best of your ability.

Let's go back to the example of housing. Just before deciding to embark on the journey of home ownership, I heard that whisper, this time encouraging me to show gratitude for where I currently lived.

Whilst some say that decorating rental properties is a complete waste of time and energy, I vehemently disagree. Sitting and stewing in a space you already aren't that fond of because you can't quite yet see the pathway to the housing situation of your dreams will create more energy blockages than I care to describe.

Whilst the changes you make should, of course, be smart all round (like: let's not go knocking down walls), I found simple things like using removable wallpaper, painting walls and having a gardener tend to our outdoor spaces had remarkable effects, not just for the energy of our home but also for my mental health. Suddenly, heading home after a long day didn't feel as if I were serving a prison sentence – I was actually relaxed. And it showed up in the work I created at the time. There was a small space next to the kitchen which was promoted as a 'dining room' which to be honest would only have been comfortable for a couple – not a family of four.

Instead of letting it become a magnet for odds and ends, I decided to turn it into a makeshift office that, decorated with bold floral wallpaper, became the hub where I wrote what went on to be *The Sunday Times* bestseller *I Am Not Your Baby Mother*. That space that I had once hated was the birthplace for work that continues to not only teach and entertain, but also create work for others.

I am forever thankful that I listened to the call to not only feel but *show* gratitude for what was then my current circumstance.

A bit like meditation, gratitude doesn't need to be grand. I would encourage you to begin simply. Start every day with a moment of stillness for gratitude and as you grow comfortable with that, think of ways you can show gratitude across the various areas of your life.

You can buy flowers for yourself or your home. Both of these show gratitude to yourself and your surroundings, but they also contribute to the pillars of Wealth, Love and Happiness that I am going to tell you about in Part 2.

You have decided to trust that spending money will come back to you.

You have decided to invest in self-love.

And when you pass by a beautiful thing you have brought into your space, that too will increase your happiness.

This was a surprise to me, but practising gratitude over the years has reminded me of the difference between wants and needs. I'll say it again: we live in a society that makes big bank by making us confuse the two. No one needs more than three pairs of shoes, to develop a sprawling wardrobe is a want. It's not necessarily a want that is wrong, but oftentimes we get so bent out of shape reaching for what we want that it blocks us from seeing how many, if not all of our needs have already been met. In order to move up a level in manifestation, we must first feel and show gratitude for what we already have.

And then sometimes gratitude works a little too well . . .

Sometimes, I become so grateful for a thing or scenario that I am currently experiencing that the yearning for what I believed to be a 'better' version of it begins to dissolve, until I almost forget about it. And then just like that – because this is how passive manifestation works – it ends up finding its way to me anyhow. (See pages 180–4 for an example of this.)

I'm telling you, gratitude is the gift that keeps on giving.

🔑 SCRIPTING

If it is said that 'the pen is mightier than the sword' then the power of scripting is exactly that: a power. Write it down.

I want to be crystal clear: scripting is not journaling.

To journal is to recount what has already happened.

Scripting is writing what will happen.

Don't get me wrong – there is room for journaling, as it acts as a way for us to purge ourselves of difficult moments, document happier ones and is a great way to reflect on our emotional growth. But, when it comes to manifestation:

Writing about your future is always going to trump dwelling on your past.

Because we are friends now, let me embarrass myself a likkle (to use Jamaican patois) piece. Recently I found a notebook that contained a story that I wrote in my early twenties about my present-day self.

I can vaguely remember writing it, and I can clearly remember the heartbreak that inspired it.

In this story, I described my current relationship in detail, the home I currently live in and even the fact I am working on projects similar to the ones I am working on now. I was confident enough not to include some people in the script at all and, lo and behold, those people are now nowhere to be found in my life today.

Almost fifteen years ago, when I wrote that short story, flooded with emotion, I had no idea what scripting was. I had no under-standing of how powerful it was to write about myself and my lifestyle as if my dreams had already transpired.

Since learning to master my own personal power, I have used scripting to support all my manifestations. As aforementioned, the key to making this tool as powerful as possible is to write as though the manifestation has already come to pass:

'I am going to' **must become** 'I am.'

'I will' **must become** 'I have.'

'I might' **must become** 'I do.'

As a child, you would have been encouraged to begin with what you were going to become – *When I grow up, I am going to be an astronaut* – so it can be quite the trip, as an adult, to get your mind-set in a place to write 'I am an astronaut', especially when, as I've said, the physical realm is always going to be lagging slightly behind.

What scripting is most powerful for is throwing our subconscious into a state of thinking that our desires have already materialised. The magic of this is that it makes us experience feelings similar to when it happens in the physical. I can't help but notice that when I am scripting about living my dream life in NYC, my mood is immediately lifted. Just like it's impossible to manifest good things whilst feeling bad, it's impossible to script about our deepest desires as if they are already fulfilled without wearing a huge smile on our faces.

Where possible I would always advise that scripting be done using an actual pen and paper, instead of on a technological device. There is a more powerful connection when your brain instructs your hand to write something in your own penmanship than when a computer dictates it to script in comic sans. But, because of the physicality my spirit has set up home in, I know all too well that there can be a plethora of barriers to what I am asking of you. As a Black woman, I'm aware that many of you reading this may experience accessibility issues in doing this, and as I've stated I would like this book to be as physically inclusive as possible. So, if a digital device is all you have access to or are able to use, that will do just fine.

You can also take this one step further and use your own voice to record your script, simply by recording your voice on any personal device. The script should be the same as when you write it. Talk about your desires as if they have already transpired. Describe the person you want to become as if you are already that person.

Sometimes I like to listen to a vocal script I have recorded when I am meditating to help magnify my intentions for the chosen manifestation. The beautiful thing about recording our scripts is that we can play the recording back and hear our future selves root for our current selves at any given time. Listening to yourself speak as if things have already come to pass is a great way to massage your subconscious to find ways to bring your desires into reality.

VISION BOARDS

Now we understand how important sitting with our current selves and speaking to our future selves is to manifesting, let's think about more practical ways we can hack our subconscious.

The imagination is one of our most powerful tools, as it allows us to see things that haven't yet moved from the spiritual into the physical. But remember: it can't work the other way round; we don't see things and then imagine them. Your imagination always, always comes first.

Typically, once we are out of childhood, we aren't encouraged to use our imaginations. As soon as we are trusted with cleaning our own asses, along comes the idea that we should stop wasting our time on something as vacuous as the imagination and start believing that there is only one reality.

Undoing this falsehood is particularly difficult if you haven't been taking your imagination to the gym.

'If you don't use it, you'll lose it!' the saying goes, and the same can surely be said for the use of our imaginations.

Now, if this part of your brain is a bit like a car that has been stationary for a while, I'm not expecting you to go from blowing the dust off to flooring it down the autobahn – easy, Hamilton. You will need a warm-up period, something to get the juices flowing, and the easiest way to send yourself into activation mode is with a vision board.

Again, vision boards are nothing new, but over the past few years they have grown in such popularity that vision board parties have replaced Tupperware ones. Vision boards are the antidote to 'you can't be what you cannot see.'

To put it simply, a vision board is a collection of images (usually glued to a large piece of paper or cardboard) that represent what we would like to have, own or be. These images should make us feel happy and excited. Some vision boards consist of material things like a dream house, car or holiday; others may focus on physical desires like getting fitter or developing a different body shape. Most importantly vision boards are used as a physical catalyst to help us get excited about whatever we are working to manifest.

Indulging in the high vibrational act of creating a vision board, no matter how saccharine and reception-art-class it may seem, is a gift of time I implore you to give yourself. I use the word indulgence because it's exactly that – a sweet pool of stolen moments, where the only thing you're asking of yourself is to honour your deepest desires, without judgement.

I won't lie, the 'first' time I worked on a vision board wasn't *really* my first go at it. It wasn't until I came to write this book that I had a hearty chuckle remembering how I once turned my small but mighty bedroom into a complete vision board.

I must have been sixteen or so. As ever, I can retrace my life via addresses and at this particular time, we were living at 67 Corry Drive within the notorious Somerleyton Estate in Brixton (very much pre the oyster and champagne bars that now exist in that area of London). For those unfamiliar with the Somerleyton Estate and its imposing doomsday brutalist facade, it isn't yet viewed through the same gentrified artistic lens as the Barbican, another example of brutalist architecture. Even the estate's grey and brown colour scheme forewarned that its main function was to suck the life out of its inhabitants. We had moved across the street earlier that summer due to ASBO[1] neighbours who quite literally used to shit in our garden.

Whilst it was hard to move again – for the eighth time in five years – the silver lining for me was having my own bedroom, a joy I hadn't felt since I was twelve. It was no bigger than a coffin and I didn't yet have a bedframe, so my mattress was on the floor. With its small window looking onto an unloved concrete garden, the interior was perhaps not that dissimilar to the cells of HMP Brixton just a stone's throw away, but it was my own.

I was working part-time and a large chunk of my pay went on

_____

1 ASBOs stands for Anti-Social Behaviour Orders, civil measures introduced by Tony Blair's government in 1998 and abolished in England in 2014.

fancy pants magazines. Fridays were my favourite day because pay day meant that I could get all my 'glossies' in. The kind South Asian man in the kiosk at Brixton station took pride in helping me source all my favourite magazines.

I had piles and piles of every glossy you could think of – the more popular ones like *Vogue* and *Elle* and the 'cooler' titles like *i-D* and *Dazed & Confused*. One day, I was in my little cell of a bedroom looking at the walls. Due to my current home not being permanent, I knew asking my parent to paint the walls would be a waste of time. My eyes fell on my stacks of old magazines.

Eureka!

Armed with multiple packs of Blu Tack and all the time in the world, I essentially wallpapered my room with images torn out of those magazines. I found myself drawn to the beautiful adverts and editorial shoots, all of which showed a life that couldn't have been more different to the one I was living on the most notorious council estate south of the river.

By the time the sun went down, I was exhausted but happy. Yes, the room was still tiny, and I was still sleeping on a mattress, but as I scanned the room, all my eyes could see was everything I wanted to have, be and feel.

As harsh and sometimes outright dangerous as the outside world could be, getting back to that small but perfect space would do something to me.

Falling asleep and waking up to visuals that made me feel positive was ground-breaking, even if I didn't yet have the language to describe vision boarding, let alone manifesting. But craning my neck and looking back almost twenty years, that's exactly what I was doing. At that time, I was existing within a life-sized vision board.

Over a decade later, by the time I came to do a much smaller version of that vision board, I had forgotten my teenage bedroom and so felt incredibly silly. I hadn't fussed with a glue stick since nursery school, and cutting into pricey magazines (I still hadn't kicked the habit) sent my lack of abundance ass into a tailspin.

But the urge to call into reality what I knew to be true and real for a different version of myself overrode any feelings of idiocy in that moment. And, most importantly, when I set the judgement of myself aside, I had to admit that this was fun.

Sitting with my legs akimbo, surrounded by a sea of magazines, I went to town, ripping, slicing and cutting pages like a lion who had just been presented with a fresh zebra after a thirty-day fast. What I clocked immediately was that I wasn't only drawn to items, such as a handbag that was currently out of my price range, but I was also drawn to imagery that communicated a *feeling*.

One thing I've noticed that people do with vision boards is that they focus on images that display something they want, but they don't necessarily think about creating a vision board that makes them feel a certain way.

Let me explain.

Seeing a model outstretched on a sun lounger rooted in the whitest sand framed by the clearest aquamarine ocean? Sure, on the surface that represented how much I wanted to experience travel, but just beneath that I noticed how the image made me *feel*: calm, relaxed and at peace.

A picture of a person at the top of a mountain after completing a hike? Again, the first point of desire was to get fit and feel good again, but the feeling that image gave me was one of accomplishment.

Images of groups of friends drinking wine and enjoying each other's company? Yes, please. Because that image made me feel as though I was part of a loving community.

It's important to understand that the first few times you make a vision board, you will definitely come up against limiting beliefs, some of which I bet you didn't even realise you had.

The first time I indulged there were certain images that called to me that I passed over, as for some reason I wasn't quite yet ready to believe I was worthy of owning such a thing or embracing how good the experience it represented might make me feel.

Not only is this perfectly fine, but it is also encouraged. To really uncover each potential block, we must first be willing to admit that there is something in our way. And as I will continue to reiterate, this practice will be harder for some of us than others.

Vision boarding has now become a practice that I commit to at least twice a year. These days my desires are usually on a very quick turnaround and so in order to vibrate on the highest level, I've got to keep those visuals up to date.

The biggest mistake I see people make with vision boards is that they assume that gazing at these images is going to magically transform their lives. I'll tell you for free, you don't automatically get to pass Go and you do not get to collect $200.

Do you remember when I said this was going to be work?

You want to collate a group of images that remind you *why* you should go out for that jog, *why* you should take steps to getting creative about the ways in which you can gain extra income and *why* you should meet up with your friends once a month.

Once we have been inspired, we still need to take action.

Doubling back for a second, I would particularly like to encourage my Black readers to spend time thinking about the feeling connected to the thing that they are trying to manifest. I have found over the course of my manifestation journey that, being a Black woman who initially came from small means, I was tricked into believing that the physical items I desired would be the source of my happiness, comfort or, most importantly for me, freedom.

I won't bullshit you, I love a good outfit so I will never *not* have an item of clothing on my vision board. But you will soon come to realise that those items and the feelings you thought they would fill you with often arrive separately.

In a society governed by capitalism and mindless consumption there is no need to chastise ourselves for having to learn that the act of acquiring a new thing won't give us the feeling we are actually searching for (typically attention, acceptance or love). Few things leave me as disgruntled as the adage: 'Money doesn't buy happiness.'

But I'll leave you to read on to get greater understanding about how I feel about that.

HOW TO VISION BOARD

There is no wrong way to vision board. Like scripting (see pages 63–5), I will always encourage you to do what is best for you as I can appreciate that access and ability issues can be a hurdle for some. Of course you can make a vision board the old-fashioned way but thankfully there is now the option to use a computer, tablet or phone to build a vision board too. If you do choose to use a device, there are so many apps at your disposal (Pinterest, Canva and Visuapp to name just a few) to help you create your digital vision board. What I love most about these is, they can come with us on the go. I've often used a digital vision board as the screensaver for my phone and laptop. I use those devices all the time, and it's nice to be greeted by my desires multiple times a day. So, whether you're using Pritt Stick or Pinterest, be comforted by the fact that as long as you clap eyes on your vision board often, it's going to have the same effect.

RIDE SOLO

If this is your first time vision boarding, I would suggest finding some time to work alone, even if it feels like it might be fun to invite a friend along. Reason being we are subconsciously very sensitive to the words and thoughts of others in moments like these. I wouldn't want a friend of yours to pass a comment that may make you feel as if you're doing it wrong or 'aiming too high'.

MUSIC MATTERS

I speak more about the importance of a soundtrack later on (see pages 206–8) but for now I want you to create a playlist that puts you on the highest vibration while you make your vision board. I would suggest steering away from anything your local bootcamp gym class would play and lean into music that feels like a nice warm hug.

ACCEPTANCE

If this is your first time approaching the exercise of vision boarding, I want you remain in a limitless childlike state for as long as possible. Pin and stick like no one is watching. Allow your subconscious to run free and really collect imagery that makes you feel as if you are on top of the world.

YOU CANNOT BE WHAT YOU CANNOT SEE!

Like all the tools, you have to commit to engaging with them regularly in order to get the most out of them. In the beginning of your manifestation journey I am going to need you to keep this vision board front and centre. If you live alone, I suggest sticking it up in a room in your home that you frequent multiple times a day. If you share space with others and you feel quite protective of your desires (this is perfectly OK, by the way), then yes, tuck it away, but be sure to set a daily reminder on your phone or calendar to take glances at it when you are able. You are trying to keep the vibrations high for as long as you can. The more you look at this vision board, the happier you should feel. This board should act as inspiration to remind you to actively work towards your desires. This isn't no hocus pocus, sweetie. What I notice a lot of people do in the first instance is they create a vision board and . . . that's it. Instead of constantly reviewing the board to remind them of how good they feel about their vison of the future, they sit back and wait for the vision board to do the work for them. That's not how it goes.

First you let the vision board inspire. Then you get ready to perspire.

KEEP IT UP TO DATE!

As you find yourself achieving one of the desires on your vision board, be ready to replace that thing with something new. Think of this like the grown-up version of a sticker chart. You best believe that your inner child wants you to fill that thing all the way up!

CRYSTALS AND CLEANSING

I have to admit, I almost didn't include these tools. If you are only just coming around to the idea of manifestation, these tools could be far too 'woo woo' for you. And yet, if I am being honest about all the tools I use in my manifesting life, there is no way I can leave out the use of crystals and herbs for energy cleansing. If this feels like a step too far for you right now, please feel free to leave these out of your toolbox until whenever, if ever, you feel called to access the highest version of you, as using crystals and herbs is definitely something I would classify as 'deeper work'. This is for when you really want to step it up a gear.

My use of both crystals and cleansing is ultimately to:

Change the energy.

You know when you step into a place, and you can just sense 'bad vibes'? Even those of us who don't believe in the supportive nature of crystals or cleansing can agree that we have all felt that feeling. Well, the use of crystals and using certain herbs to 'cleanse' a space can for sure make a difference in those 'off key' moments.

I've been around crystals my whole life. They were often displayed as pieces of art on the mantelpieces and dressing tables of my childhood, with some women who were close to me growing up even sporting them as jewellery. I know for sure most of those people never knew the power of crystals and they certainly had very little understanding of manifestation, if any at all. But I was always drawn to crystals, without knowing how much I would go on to use them in my day-to-day life.

As I've matured in my spiritual journey, I have found myself interacting with crystals every single day. If I remember correctly, someone gifted me with a heart-shaped rose quartz shortly after I gave birth to my daughter. They mentioned its properties (which include the promotion of compassion, forgiveness, healing and self love), which made me curious about where crystals come from and what many believe their purpose to be.

Whilst I'm not a crystallographer, I think it's important to give you a brief education about this particular tool. Nature gives birth to crystals when molten rock starts to cool and harden, and certain molecules convene to stabilise in a process called crystallisation. As with all things, crystals start small but as more atoms are drawn together, the crystal starts to grow. All things on earth carry energy, and crystals are no different. Each crystal, just like us, carries its own vibrational frequency as well as being jam-packed with the energy of the universe around us. What I personally like about crystals is how they act as a veil between science and spirit.

Over time I have used crystals to support me in multiple ways. When I was pregnant with my second child, a sound healer gifted me with a 'midwife stone', more commonly known as malachite. Alongside practising hypnobirthing, that crystal became as important to me as my maternity notes; fiddling with it helped keep me calm.

Many spiritual teachers who use crystals advise that if you lose a crystal or it breaks, it has simply done its job. A week after my son was born, the midwife stone fell out of my handbag and smashed to pieces. I had been working with crystals long enough to not feel saddened, but to accept that the stone had done all it needed to do for me.

Today, there isn't a nook or cranny in my home where you won't find crystals. I have a huge wand of selenite (good for cleaning out stagnant energy) on my dressing room island, a piece of citrine (encourages prosperity) in my purse, a tray filled with rose quartz, black obsidian (the protector) and amethyst (great for spiritual healing and wisdom) to the left of me as I write this, and I've often been caught off guard when clothes shopping as I forget that I often keep a few tumbling stones in my bra. Literally crystals are everywhere.

But I have to be clear, I don't believe the crystals alone will work miracles for me, nor are they the tool I would reach for first. They seem to be most powerful when used in conjunction with other tools and practices I'll cover later in this book, but it would have felt cheeky to not give them a much-deserved honourable mention first.

The same can be said for cleansing, which is the act of using herbs (typically sage), incense or essential oils to clear out stagnant or negative energy from a space. Cleansing has roots across many cultures dating back almost five thousand years. It is recorded that even ancient Egyptians used to cleanse with sage.

I typically like to energetically 'cleanse' a space with either sage or the sacred wood Palo Santo, the latter being my personal favourite due to its beautiful scent. I do this by burning the sage or Palo Santo and moving around every room in home, whilst asking for negative energy to leave and positive energy to come in. Dependent upon how I'm feeling and who is home, this verbal request can swing from a whisper to low shout. I always have some windows open as I want the negative energy and the smoke to go somewhere. I find I am drawn to cleanse my space when I or another member of the household feels a bit 'off', whether they are having bad dreams, or they are physically unwell. And I always cleanse after having visitors who've stayed the night. It's become so habitual to me that I see this version of cleansing as no different to changing bed linen and towels after guests have left. Whilst my personal preferences are Palo Santo and sage there are many other plants to choose from including rosemary, sandalwood and Yerba Santa.

I can remember going to elders' homes and the pungent smell of incense greeting me before anyone opened the door. If I questioned my 'aunties' or 'uncles' about the herbs they chose, they would simply tell me to stay out of grown folks' business. Now that I'm grown folk myself, I know it was their way of encouraging negative energy to leave whilst inviting positive energy in.

In my day-to-day life, I cleanse if I think there is an energy of lack or fear, or I feel a block to positive energy. Whenever I have moved home, before the first box is even unpacked, I whip out a new bundle of the herb of my choice and get to work at cleansing the space, which was once a physical and spiritual home to others and their energies.

As with all things manifestation-related, your intention when cleansing is more important than the act itself.

When cleansing we can use ALL the tools to support our desires.

For instance, you can use ASKfirmations whilst walking slowly around your new space.

Why am I so happy here?

Why is this home the perfect place to put down roots?

What wonderful things will the safe space encourage me to create?

You can also cleanse your space before meditation, which will help you get in a more relaxed, quiet mood.

You can cleanse whilst expressing **gratitude.**

You can cleanse before a session of **scripting** or **vision boarding.**

You can even clean your crystals with these herbs! Yes, you read that correctly. You can use a smoke of your choice to set intentions over used or new crystals, either of which will have picked up a plethora of energetic flows before ending up with you.

May I also suggest that with herbs and crystals alike, if at all possible you purchase them in real life. I cannot tell you how many times I have had to ask people to think about the energy involved with making certain purchases. Using a bundle of sage purchased from Amazon is not the best start – it is more than likely that those herbs have passed through a negative energy space.

Whenever you can, I would encourage you to purchase anything to support your manifestation work from a small business that your intuition tells you puts positivity before profit. As ever, I understand that there could be accessibility issues to you investing in crystals and herbs, so I want to reassure you that, whilst they can be great components to supporting your manifestation practices, you don't need them to begin.

PART 2

The Four Pillars

To prevent this book from becoming a saga – as there is so much I could say about manifestation – I thought it was best to break down the areas in which most people tend to want to manifest into four 'pillars'. These are:

Wellness

Wealth

Love

Happiness

Without question, most of our desires can be filed under at least one of the above. Sometimes what we wish to come true is an intersection of two or more. And if you really want to push the boat out, what we want most for our lives can touch all four.

I have come to notice that those who feel best about their lives have, to some degree, come to a place of acceptance and peace with all four pillars. This is not to say that these pillars are always in perfect shape, or that events don't sometimes shake the overall foundation, but rather that, generally speaking, all four pillars are strong enough to allow the person to feel that their life is well supported and they are able to flourish.

I want to explain how important it is to recognise that, even though these pillars stand alone, the instability of one can have a detrimental effect on the others.

I have listed wellness as the first pillar as, if you don't feel well, the other three pillars are in danger of toppling over. If you are feeling unwell, be that mentally, physically or both, it is hard to concentrate on your work, which can have a knock-on effect on your finances and that's the wealth pillar thrown over.

When our body 'fails' us it can be difficult to practice self-love because our bodies aren't currently following our orders. This will, of course, throw us into a low vibration. And don't go thinking that, just because these vibrations are invisible, they aren't powerful. They are, as my Jamaican grandmother would say in patois, 'likkle but tallawah' (which loosely translates as something being small but mighty). These vibrations cannot be lied to, and as the Law of Attraction dictates, we can only receive what we give out.

So, with that in mind, if we are struggling to love ourselves, it may be hard to express love for others. So that's the love pillar out the game.

Honestly, I feel as though the final pillar – happiness – is self-explanatory. If you currently feel well, I want you to cast your mind back to when you were last unwell, I mean truly out for the count. For me it was two Christmases ago, when I couldn't leave my bed for a week. I don't know about you, but I felt every emotion apart from happiness. It was a heady mix of anger and self-pity as I had to commit my body to bed and let the joyful sounds of the Christmas holidays waft up the stairs and into my bedroom, which resembled a hospital suite.

In a far more concise way, the same could be said for the wealth pillar. If a person feels as though they don't have access to enough means to allow them to meet their basic human needs, then every other pillar is rendered useless. They cannot work or love comfortably. And in the case of the wellness pillar, in many places on this earth if a person doesn't have enough funds at their disposal for healthcare, their lives can truly hang in the balance. I speak from deep experience when I say that when the dark cloud of financial woes hangs over your head, even drizzle can feel like a tornado. But more on that later.

When it comes to the love pillar, I often ask, 'Well, what is life without love?' Love is without doubt one of the most powerful human emotions (unfortunately, the only one that pips it to the post is hate). To love and be loved has, throughout the history of humanity, been the thing that moves all.

We have watched kings turn their backs on wealth and prestige for it.

We have seen people make the error of thinking they can buy it.

And for various reasons, we have even watched people die for it.

I would say that, in my personal experience, if this pillar is neglected it can skew the true intent of our manifestations as sometimes what we imagine to be one of our deep desires is in fact making up for a lack of love in our lives.

Nothing can.

Of course, there are multiple versions of love, and many ways to give and receive love, so we shouldn't buy into the falsehood that the only way to build this pillar is through romantic love. Some of the greatest love stories of my life thus far have been platonic. And when all is said and done, the vibration isn't going to be affected because of how love came to be; love simply needs to be present.

Happiness is a bit of a renegade; some would argue that once the other three pillars are strong enough, this final one should take care of itself. But this is far from the truth. I think we can all agree that we know people who are in good health but unhappy. Who have more money than they know what to do with, yet still feel despair. And, of course, there are those who feel love from an audience of millions, yet who still cry themselves to sleep at night. Happiness is a pillar in and of itself that needs just as much activation and aftercare as the other three. In fact, I would go as far to say this is perhaps the pillar you should concentrate on the most, as this is the one that sparks feeling.

If you remember nothing else, remember that in order to manifest *anything*, you must feel it before you see it.

You do not get what you ask for.
You get what you are.

If the happiness pillar is the strongest, that will help with building up the other three, as you can lean on the positive vibrations that this pillar emits, transferring any excess good energy to the other pillars which aren't yet as strong.

Just like your manifestations, your dependence upon the pillars can also be intersectional. You will very likely find that you are leaning on a few pillars at a time in order to bring a desire to fruition.

I can appreciate that there may be one pillar in your life giving you more concern than others, so you are perhaps tempted to skip to that pillar and get stuck in. May I suggest you don't do that?

What my manifesting journey has taught me thus far is that there is something to be learned in each pillar of my life that will have great use for the others. I don't want you to miss that magic, which can make your manifestation more bountiful, just because you decided to focus on one pillar of your life more than the other.

The pillars are all equal and inter dependent.

To ignore one could lead to the detriment of them all.

◉ WELLNESS

Buckle up, buttercup: we are going on one hell of a ride. My journey with personal wellness has been a steep climb. As you will find out through this chapter, what presented as physical symptoms for me then led to an understanding of how deeply physical and spiritual wellness are intertwined.

But first things first, and as a reminder of how much I'm not invested in selling you bullshit, I want to be transparent about what this book *won't* do. (Perhaps because publishers fear it wouldn't sell, I have yet to come across a manifestation book that is clear about its limitations.)

It will not cure cancer.

It will not reverse paralysis.

It will not make depression disappear.

It will not completely erase the symptoms of chronic illness.

It will not be the answer to eternal life.

It will not prevent death.

It will not bring your loved ones back from the dead.

The reason I must begin here is because I would never want anyone either to depend on manifestation alone, or to think that what I say can be used in place of what a doctor prescribes. That is rubbish. And I can confidently say that any other manifestation material that says it can do any of the above is rubbish too.

The tools and lessons shared in this book should always be used in tandem with whatever healthcare treatment is available – they cannot be relied upon as the cure. But what I share here *can* encourage the energy that is necessary for living as positive a life as you can, *regardless* of your current physical circumstance. And that is something I think we can all agree that we desire.

So, let's begin.

As ever, your intention must be clear.

WHAT DOES WELLNESS MEAN TO YOU?

For most of you, the word wellness will bring up thoughts solely around your physical health. For others it will mean feeling secure not just in your body but also in your mind. For a few of you, there may be a pause here, because you've never had a reason or the time to think about wellness at all. Aside from trying to avoid catching a cold or nursing a hangover, your interaction with the word 'wellness' might be very limited. Don't worry, all levels are accepted here.

Personally, to me, **wellness means striving to exist in my most optimum physical, mental and spiritual state.**

I use the word striving because I have had to accept that my personal scale of optimum wellness is always in flux.

I know I am at optimum wellness when my physical, mental and spiritual states are all in flow. Those three states don't feel clogged or heavy, and they are all in harmony with one another. As an example, during the editing process of this book my wellness pillar needed some reinforcement as I had a tooth extraction that led to dry socket. I was once again reminded how easy it is for my physical state to have a knock-on effect on my mental and spiritual state. If you've never had dry socket, then thank your lucky stars. Both times I've been the lucky recipient of the dry socket award, I have said that I would honestly much rather have had more C-sections. Even gently breathing hurts. The pain is so all-consuming, you can't even think about anything else, let alone trying to stay mentally positive.

Like most, I think I take umbrage with the term 'wellness' because of how so many practices linked to 'being well' have been colonised and turned into capitalist opportunities. I see advertisements working hard to convince us that to drink from the fountain of wellness, we must empty our pockets.

In my own community, I've seen the use of certain herbs and other nutrient-rich ingredients that my grandparents and great-grandparents used to help ease symptoms and ailments be cornered by a western market. Nowadays, products that we could once have acquired either for free or for very little are sold at an egregious price.

So, before bobbing and weaving through this section, I want to make one thing clear:

It shouldn't cost the earth to feel well.

In fact, I'd argue that the earth would say, it shouldn't cost anything at all.

If ever you feel pressured to put wellness on a credit card, I want you to think deeply about who is telling you this is needed, and why.

Most wellness practices do not need a price tag attached.

No matter what your state of health, there are many supportive tools you can use to manifest a version of personal wellness that you can maintain on your own terms.

THE PRACTICE: **YOUR OPTIMUM WELLNESS**

To help you figure out what your version of optimum wellness might be, think of the last time you felt as though your physical, spiritual and mental needs were all met. What was going on during that time? What did your support system look like? What practices did you have in place to help support your wellness?

If you can pinpoint this time, the next thing to do is to recognise what has changed between then and now. Is there any way you can replicate elements of the time when you felt you were at optimum wellness?

WHEN THE BODY SPEAKS

Although my family history of mental health issues may mean I struggle for a lifetime (more on that later), physically I come from a relatively healthy bloodline.

On both sides of my family, members live well into their eighties, with most of their health ailments caused by the wear and tear of time. The few anomalies that have occurred have luckily always been diagnosed in a time frame that allowed the person to seek the necessary healthcare, and they then went on to a live long, healthy life.

But then there are the members who have sadly, due to illness, died prematurely. For me, the latter has been an experience that has cut deeply.

When I was twenty, my father passed away from complications arising from the common flu. To be clear, this was in 2009, well before Covid, when we weren't all aware of how deadly influenza can be if not taken seriously. He declined so quickly – within three days – that by the time he took himself to A&E at Whipps Cross Hospital – still hoping to head off afterwards to see his beloved Arsenal FC play later that day – he went into cardiac arrest in the waiting area, and was pronounced dead ten minutes later.

Somewhere in southern Italy, his only child was about to receive news that would not only change the entire trajectory of her life, but also open a can bursting full of health anxiety.

The pains began perhaps six months after he died. They started in my joints and then seemed to flood my limbs. Many days it felt as though my entire body was on fire. This, coupled with crippling exhaustion, made me feel sure that I would join my dad soon. I felt as though my body didn't belong to me at all.

Between grief and trying to balance my new reality, advocating for myself was quite a struggle. It would be another eighteen months and multiple GP and hospital appointments until my childhood doctor was able to help me understand what was going on.

Sighing, I flopped into the chair I had been surrendering my body to since I was primary school age.

Dr Lee was a slight Chinese man. His office was decorated with cosy vibes in mind; one couldn't help but assume that this space was a detailed reflection of what his personal interior space would look like.

Whilst the other doctors at this surgery made good with whatever furniture was available, Dr Lee clearly liked his shit to be custom. A deep-toned mahogany desk sat between us like a physical reminder of the required doctor-patient boundary. Behind him, large mahogany bookcases heaved under a selection of books with titles too long for me to read. The chair I sat in hugged me perfectly, almost tricking me into believing that I was about to chop it up with a friend.

Finally, Dr Lee always had incense burning. Stepping into his office, leaving the busy panic of the waiting room that buzzed with the sounds of hacking coughs and a constantly ringing phone felt . . . tranquil. And that's perhaps why Dr Lee had the longest roster of patients. We in the local community had known for years that he never adhered to the unspoken rule of getting through patients as fast as possible. Each appointment took as long as he believed it should, which meant that, without fail, he was late for the next patient. But no one complained, because ultimately everyone wanted to be seen by a doctor who made you feel as though you were safe in their care.

'OK, Dr Lee, hit me with it,' I snapped, already tensing my body for the next level of fuckery that I was sure the universe was about to send my way.

'I don't have a bat in here, Candice,' he responded, before bursting into his usual fit of childish giggles.

I allowed myself to loosen up.

'I'm happy to report that all your blood tests have come back normal. But having spoken with my colleagues, I do think you're suffering with something called fibromyalgia.'

My mind was racing.

'Now given the history of your family's mental health, I think . . .'

'Dr Lee! Slow down, man.' I cut in, 'What's fibro . . .' I trailed off, not wanting to embarrass myself.

'Yes, goodness me, I often forget what a patient doesn't know. Fibromyalgia is a long-term condition with a variety of symptoms, including the pain you've been describing and the tiredness. The reasons I've come to this diagnosis are: number one, all your tests have been fine – this usually happens with fibromyalgia – but secondly and most importantly, it's usually triggered by something, including stress. And I don't think that would be absurd given what . . .' It was his turn to trail off.

I swallowed hard and looked out the window. This condition, if it needed a trigger ... what could be bigger than earth-shattering grief? After the third week of not being able to crack more than two hours of sleep a day, it had been Dr Lee who had finally agreed to prescribe sleeping aids. It was also him who had provided a referral to the local psychotherapist, insisting that I be offered sessions as a 'matter of urgency'.

I remember him saying that, given my family's mental health history, it was imperative that we used all the systems available to ensure that I stayed on the right side of this battle.

Because, whilst this was my first date with poor physical health, when it came to poor mental health? Well, I had been married to that. I came from not just a household, but a community that was full of people who struggled with their mental health, partly because of genetics and partly because of the stress of trying to succeed in oppressive environments. Growing up, it didn't help that if you were suffering mentally, the only advice anyone had was, 'Don't speak about it, pray about it.'

From a data standpoint the above approach perhaps gives a hint as to why, in the year 2022, Black people were the most likely to be detained under the Mental Health Act, with 342 detentions per 100,000 people. Yet they also received the least mental health treatment of any ethnic group. In my personal life this statistic showed up as several immediate family members being either on very strong, long-term medication to help manage their mental health conditions, or being one of those who were detained. Having witnessed family members pumped to the brim with mind-numbing medication at a psychiatric hospital in South London, I pray no one else has to see their loved one in that state.

So, whilst it felt as though I was going mad, I didn't dare show it.

But now, the low vibrational *energetic implications* of *not* sharing how I was feeling were all coming back to bite me on the ass. Our bodies are incubators, holding all that we are feeling, all of the time.

I thought to myself, 'Is this fibro-magigy-thing a physical manifestation of what I'm feeling emotionally?' I decided to slip my question into my back pocket and concentrate on what Dr Lee was saying.

'The thing is, there is no cure, *per se*,' Dr Lee mused, 'As a doctor, all I know is that there is a connection between how you feel mentally and how you feel physically that must be respected.'

That was a far quicker answer than I was looking for.

'So, what now? What will you give me?' I asked, trying to moderate the begging tone that was pushing forth.

'I think the correct answer is, what will you give yourself? On my end I can give you pain medication, and we can definitely explore physical therapy, but to be honest the more pressing issue is: how can we help you manage your stress?'

And that is how working on my wellness began. With me researching how I could perhaps, on the most wishful end, heal myself, but on the other, most realistic end, achieve the bare minimum, which was to manage my disease by managing my stress.

This was not an overnight process. In fact, it took a few years, with the first and hardest hurdle being: movement.

MOVEMENT

When it comes to manifestation, movement is one of the most powerful things you can do.

I realised that languishing in my pain was a trigger for more pain. Now this isn't to say that a switch in my head flipped, and I was suddenly able to jump out of bed like a Duracell bunny, but it does mean that I found movement, no matter how small, to be an entry-way to both lessening my physical pain and offering some mental respite.

Being in pain and not being physically able to utilise our bodies are not always a package deal. **There are times when pain may restrict our movement, but that doesn't mean it has robbed us entirely of the liberty to move.**

There are of course times where our physical pain or chronic illness will arrest us and all we can do is listen to the command of being still.

But in my own instance, there were slight breaks in the pain that I wasn't utilising at all. Much like the contractions I would experience years later when giving birth, there were moments between those tight cramps, where it would feel as though all was well. In labour, during the moments between contractions I even found myself laughing with those in the delivery room before the next wave took me. That is how it felt with fibromyalgia, especially upon waking. Often first thing it felt as if my brain hadn't yet had time to register what was to come, and I learned that I could seize those moments.

The simple act of moving generates more of the desired energy.

And so, I began simply with walking. Always an early riser, I challenged myself to get up before the sun and walk a mile. Over the years I've learned that the time I choose to lean into movement is important. If I push it until later in the day, it simply won't get done. I had no desire to power walk, let alone run; walking was simply my way of telling my body that I wasn't always going to succumb to the pain. Where possible, I wanted to use movement to send a different message to my brain.

THE 'SCIENCE'

Even a gentle walk triggers the release of important hormones: oxytocin, endorphins, serotonin and dopamine. These 'magic making' hormones not only make us feel happier, but also reduce stress, anxiety and depression.

But it doesn't end there. Moving your body triggers the release of myokines. These are small proteins that are released by our muscle fibres into the bloodstream during exercise. Myokines change the structure of our brains and have a similar effect to antidepressants. Scientists have nicknamed these myokines 'Hope Molecules'.

Years later, I wasn't that surprised when I was encouraged to get up a few hours after having an emergency C-section. Fibromyalgia had already shown me how important it was to promote an atmosphere of healing through movement.

Thousands of studies have shown how exercise (no matter how low impact) can improve our moods and reduce stress.

THE PRACTICE: **GENTLY DOES IT**

When trying to feel better (especially physically) you must **expect** and then **accept** that in the first instance, there may be a short period where you feel a little worse. But it is vital to try and make the most of the slivers of pain-free time that we are gifted. It is during these moments that we can shift our energy from victim to victorious.

This time need not be exhaustive. When working your way back to physical wellness, you simply need to begin with five minutes. You can increase the time as you feel better.

It's imperative to start slowly, and take it gently, so you don't do more damage than good.

What movement is possible for you right now?

Since being diagnosed with fibromyalgia, I have returned to the power of movement time and time again to help manifest my personal wellness. Of course, this is an undulating practice and there have been seasons where I have not engaged in as much movement as necessary and I have had to pay the price for neglect, especially when it came to my mental health.

One thing bouts of ill health have also taught me is to be clear and upfront about what I *cannot* do at that present time. Whilst I was writing this book, I decided to commit to one year of learning to run again. After successfully completing 300 runs over the course of 365 days – something I would once never have believed possible – a mentor of mine reached out and offered me a place in the 2024 London Marathon. My ego wanted to grab that offer with both hands. I had previously run the London Marathon years before so it wasn't hard for me to close my eyes and feel the magic of it all, the elation of crossing the finish line, reaching mile twenty-one with all my supporters cheering me on. But another part of me, thankfully a more mature part, simply said, 'Thank you. But I'm not ready yet.' Even I, with all my manifesting prowess, have learned that it's OK to admit when you aren't ready to do something because the foundation isn't ready.

So, I am not discouraging you from running a marathon one day – maybe that is a future goal for you – but if right now all you can manage is a slow walk to the corner shop, I am telling you to show gratitude to be living in a body that is able to follow your commands. Heck, I demand it. There is no such thing as perfect but there is always better.

Finally, remember: movement is not a punishment, it's a privilege.

It is at this point that I want to remind you of a key manifesting idea:

You don't get what you ask for, you get what you are (and in this case, do).

We must feel it first.

What can you do to create a feeling of wellness?

You cannot simply lay in bed and say 'I am well' five times, think you're done for the day and then roll over and wait for the magic to happen. You get more of what you are, and in this case, *do*. When it comes to many aspects of health and wellness, **you** are the magic.

When we cracked open the magic toolbox for the first time (see pages 23–82), I pointed out that the tools would always be strongest when used together. The same trick applies here.

Over time, as my short walks began to make me feel a little stronger, I decided to introduce affirmations into my walking time. (I wasn't yet aware of how much more suited I was for ASKfirmations – and to be frank it didn't matter.) These walks, coupled with me mentally repeating phrases like:

'I am well.'

'I am in control.'

I am free from pain medication'.

... were the only medicines my body needed. If you are now working through your own health journey, I would encourage you to turn those phrases in to ASKfirmations.

THE PRACTICE: **ASKFIRMATIONS FOR WELLNESS**

Whilst engaging in movement you enjoy, ask yourself:

'Why am I well?'

'How am I in control?'

'What does life look like now I am free from pain medication?'

TUNING IN

Now let's focus on the practice of listening to our bodies.

We live in such a fast-paced, noisy world. And sometimes we struggle to even find a moment of peace in our own homes. Trust me, I get it. As I currently type this question, I'm sat on the sofa with my entire family. My husband and daughter are playing a VERY loud video game on the TV. My son is on his tablet, intermittently raising his head to offer direction on the game and my needy chihuahua, Brixton, is so close to me I can feel his heartbeat. This, or a version of this, will be a familiar situation for many of you reading this book.

'**How do you know what your body is trying to say, if you never make time to listen to it?**'

Because you better believe our bodies are always talking to us.

Pain shouts the loudest and is always a sign that physically we aren't in alignment and should investigate further. But loud pain isn't always the way the body says something is wrong; you can also simply feel 'off'. This signal is far harder to notice than pain, which is why the practice of meditation (see pages 43–53) when trying to either maintain optimum health or work our way back to wellness, is so important.

Meditation encourages you to quiet your mind and make space for what else could be happening within.

GOOD MORNING HYGIENE

Since being diagnosed with fibromyalgia, working through my flare-ups has taught me that, for me, optimum wellness begins with a Good Morning Hygiene practice. No, I'm not talking about brushing your teeth for a minimum of three minutes, although I'm sure whoever you're in communication with will greatly appreciate your efforts on that front.

Do you have Good Morning Hygiene? I'm talking about how you start your day.

Expecting a feel-good day if you start with poor morning hygiene is the energetic equivalent of trying to drive a car that has no petrol in the tank. In order to manifest wellness, you must commit to developing the habit of starting your day in the best way possible.

I'm going to share my current morning routine. Don't worry, it isn't the ninety-minute, appliance-ridden affair we are sold via social media. All you need are seven to ten minutes.

Firstly, the way you are pulled from sleep to waking is important. So, let's begin with alarm sounds. For years, I allowed myself to be woken up suddenly and aggressively. My choice of a harsh alarm sound would slice through my sleep like a sword, jolting me awake. I would jump up, sure that I needed to fight for my life.

Using an alarm like this encourages an immediate spike in cortisol, a stress hormone that can have negative effects on our health over time. Since choosing a more gradual, softer alarm sound, I have found that I don't awaken on high alert. It allows me to be pulled into the new day more gently.

When possible, I don't allow the use of an alarm at all and far prefer to be in tune with nature and allow the expanding light from sunrise to nudge me gently out of my slumber. I call this the Soft Stir.

If you can, I would encourage the use of an alarm clock over the use of a mobile phone. Reason being, I don't want to be tempted into interacting with my phone so early in the morning. We have the rest of our waking hours to interact with screens, let's give ourselves a minute.

Before I even allow my feet to touch the floor, I then move into my Gratitude Greeting. This does what it says on the tin: it's a way to greet your day with gratitude. Remember how powerful I explained gratitude to be in your magic toolbox (see pages 55–62)? Its power very much applies here. I would suggest that during this hygiene practice that you actually DON'T use a pen and paper – or a phone. You want to delay the urge to *do* for as long as possible and allow yourself to just *be*. All that is required of you is to make a silent, mental note of whatever you choose to be grateful for.

Gratitude is such a powerfully energetic tool, and particularly so when it's the primary feeling you choose to begin your day with. Long after I've made my morning Gratitude Greeting, I can find myself being grateful for what others would deem the simplest of things. Gratitude, or rather the way gratitude makes you *feel* can be addictive.

Now it's time to get out of bed. Only now, if *absolutely necessary*, will I allow myself to interact with my phone. Typically, I try to resist until I've completed the next phase, which I like to call Nurtured by Nature.

Reflecting on my initial fibromyalgia diagnosis, I have noticed that the biggest positive impact on my mental health was going outside. Now, no matter what the temperature, I begin my day by drinking a hot beverage in the garden.

When the weather permits, I like to do this barefoot.

This is known as grounding.

THE 'SCIENCE': **GROUNDING**

Everything, including you, is made up of atoms. These tiny atoms carry a neutral charge, due to the fact that they contain equal numbers of negatively charged electrons and positively charged protons. But sometimes these atoms lose an electron. If an atom has an unpaired electron, it can be a problem, turning into a free radical atom. These atoms can become capable of damaging our cells and therefore contribute to chronic illness and cancers. The amazing thing is that the ground's surface can provide the stabiliser that an unpaired atom needs as the ground is in the business of creating electrons that can neutralise these otherwise lawless atoms. Grounding can regulate our nervous systems and synchronise our circadian rhythm. In Candice-speak: sometimes we need a good recharge – and grounding can do this for us.

Grounding is an accessible and cost-free practice to help us work our way to wellness. Of course, I speak from a place of privilege given that I have access to a garden. For some of you reading, grounding may not be a practice you can access all the time, and this is fine. But whenever you can, be sure to embrace the freedom that comes with connecting with nature in this way. It is incredibly freeing.

The final thing I would like to add to this Good Morning Hygiene routine is a practice for which I've coined the phrase:

Delay is not denial.

The reason why I've added this last is because I didn't even realise this is something I practised until my husband pointed it out to me.

I do not under any circumstances engage with any news platform until at least one hour after I've woken up.

This makes for a little tension in my household, because my husband Bodé's very first request to our Amazon Echo in the mornings is 'Alexa, play LBC.' When we began living together, he was working a job that would take him away from the house an hour or two before I had to get up, so his thirst for world news first thing wasn't something I immediately noticed. But, of course, since lockdown and then his leaving that job so that we could go into business together, Bodé's desire to be met with typically bad news so early in the morning has become something we often knock heads about.

'It's important to stay informed,' he huffed one day, after I had sternly told Alexa to turn it off.

'I agree but, my word, can't it wait? Have you noticed the news is never overwhelmingly positive, is it?'

His silence was him admitting defeat.

I continued: 'Like the elders say about our blessings, a delay is not a denial. I think it's the same here. I am not saying that to be ignorant is cool, but I *will* say that holding off on what is only ever an update on how much humanity has gone to shit can only be a good thing for your mental health.'

'I hear you,' he begrudgingly admitted.

Since then, if Bodé gets to the kitchen before me, he keeps the volume very low and doesn't mind if I turn it off entirely once I get there. I know that this practice is something he doesn't care for as the kids have reported back to me that they listen to the news on the way to school and our six-year-old son can often be heard mindlessly humming the LBC theme tune. But it's clear to everyone I live with that I have boundaries about when I interact with the world news.

So, I would like to open this out by asking you to think about what vibration you allow to penetrate your atmosphere first thing in the morning. Is it depressing world news, where you find yourself having a one-sided argument with someone who has called into a current affairs show? Or do you prefer to listen to music or a podcast that uplifts you, and sets a more positive tone for the day ahead?

Over time, you will realise that manifestation is not that dissimilar to trying to keep up a healthy, nutritious diet. To glean the highest benefits, you must pay attention to all that you are allowing yourself to ingest. Like fast food, sporadic moments of low-vibrational activity won't do any harm, but for that to be the bulk of your mind's diet is going to do far more harm than good.

THE PRACTICE: **GOOD MORNING HYGIENE**

Are you giving yourself the time you need to create the foundation for a day that serves you well?

1. **Encourage the Soft Stir.** Take note of how you allow yourself to be woken up. If you use an alarm sound that panics you, try changing it to a softer, creeping sound that will slowly make you more aware.

2. **Develop your Gratitude Greeting.** Before you swing your feet to the floor, spend one to two minutes thinking of all the things you can be grateful for. I typically start by thinking how grateful I am to have made it through the night, and then I think about how grateful I am to

have woken up in a safe environment. We can up the ante on this by *showing* gratitude (see pages 55–62) by making sure we make our bed immediately. Doing so is a great way to display care for a place where you spend a large portion of your time.

3. **If you can, be Nurtured by Nature.** Where possible, before break-fast, get outside. If you have access to a back garden, get into the habit of having a hot beverage out there. If you have a balcony, utilise it. If you must walk the dog, make that the first thing you do. If you have no dog, walk yourself! Aim to spend at least ten minutes out in the open air. I also want to add here that I'm a mother of two children who are still of school age, so I appreciate that the mornings can be absolute carnage. But here is the only advice I have: to make this work you are going to have to get up ten minutes earlier. Developing these habits is going to take sacrifice no matter how you want to look at it. I'm so sorry. Kinda.

4. **Remember that Delay is not Denial.** To be clear, being ignorant about world events is not cool. Being clued up on what is happening in the world around you is imperative for developing an empathetic humanity that understands the absolute need for care and support on a local and global level. But as individuals we can temper when and how much of the world news we take in. During the peak of the pandemic, myself and perhaps many of you reading this lived with news on in the background and were constantly glued to our phones. Let's think about how that overconsumption of bad news affected us. For me, it triggered one of the worst flare-ups of fibromyalgia I've had in years. As a raging empath I often ask myself, 'Who do you think you are, to dip in and out of things when it suits you? If only those you are

receiving the information about could be so lucky.' I had to recognise that this was the wrong approach. How can I teach, heal and offer support if I am too negatively affected by all that I am consuming? Be sure that you are regulating when you decide to engage with the news, as this is for sure going to have a knock-on effect on the rest of your day.

LIVING WELL OR LIVING LONG?

How do we manifest wellness in the face of death?

Mic drop.

As a Black woman, I do not have the privilege of communicating only the more palatable parts of manifestation. My lived experience is a constant reminder about how hard life can be for someone like me, because of the body I was born into. So to write about wellness without leaving space for the inevitable feels like a lie.

People die.

We will die.

How the hell do you manifest when the only wish that you or someone you love really has is for life itself?

When writing this book, I was asked to work with Black Women Rising, a UK-based charity that supports Black women who are dealing with life during and after cancer diagnosis.

I was hesitant at first as I do not have any personal experience of cancer and hope I never will. But the founder, Leanne Pero, made it clear that the event was going to focus on how to build and retain self-love, even in the face of the most trying times.

Now, of that, I had first-hand experience.

A dear friend of mine who was diagnosed with breast cancer a few years ago warned me that I might find the event draining, as understandably many women living with cancer are exactly that – drained after having to pick up the shattered pieces of the life they thought they were going to live. What I didn't expect was to meet women who gave me a great perspective on what it means to live well, even whilst dying.

'Now, I live for today, which is what I should have been doing all along. None of us know when our last breath is coming. This diagnosis has just made me aware of that.'

'Even with this disease, I still get to determine how I live my life. Next week, instead of going through another gruelling round of chemo, I'm going to New York City! Cancer can wait!'

'Yes, I am dying. But aren't we all? Cancer has taught me how to live well.'

I left the event flooded with new ideas about how I wanted to talk about the wellness pillar. Because these women proved to me that even in ill-health, they still wanted and had a *right* to live well.

So many of the world's ideas about wellness are actually rooted in living long, not necessarily living *well*. But one of the women I met at the Black Women Rising event said it best:

'I made the decision early into my diagnosis that I would say "no" to more treatment if that meant solely prolonging my life, instead of maintaining a good quality of life. Many will say a long life and a good life are the same thing; they are not.'

For some of you reading this, this will have been a choice that you or someone close to you has had to make. Living well rather than living long might mean looking at all the options that are on offer and choosing what is best for you – not what your partner, children or friends may think is best (which, I'll be honest, having been that person at the side of the hospital bed, is often rooted in selfishness: 'I would very much like more time with this person, thank you very much'). For some of the women I met, this meant saying 'no' to more medication, because it would interfere with the quality of life they have left. For the husband of another friend, this meant choosing to live his last days at home, not in hospital.

LETTING GO

So, how can we manifest wellness under any circumstances?

By letting go.

Learning to release our expectations of *how* our desires come to fruition has been a reoccurring encouragement throughout this book.

And this is one of, if not *the* hardest thing you must get used to doing. I appreciate it feels counterintuitive because you have, of course, put so much actual energy into visualising and harnessing your desires because you want change, but often it is our resistance to allowing things to be as they are that is causing us the most difficulty.

The most powerful way to manifest is to ask, accept, expect. And then let go.

It is in letting go that Source can see that you trust all is going to work out for your betterment.

Whenever I meet someone who says they struggle with the concept of manifesting or they don't believe in it, I simply ask them if they use a diary or a calendar to plot future dates. Whether it be on a device or on paper, almost everyone employs the use of a diary to help them plan their life. I then go on to interrogate why they believe the future plans they have made, whether for a coffee date with a friend or a quarterly catch-up with their boss, will actually come to pass?

I try not to smirk when they are forced to pause.

Here's the thing, none of us know that the plans we make for the future are actually going to transpire. Yet with full confidence we block out time that we believe without a shadow of a doubt our future selves will make use of.

To drive this analogy even further home, once we have decided on this date, unless there are scheduling issues, we don't have anxiety around the thing we plan to do, we just expect it to happen. We don't harass our friends or colleagues constantly to make sure they remember the date – we just let it be.

This is exactly how manifestation works.

A bit like how many of you don't feel the need to check your bank account first thing on pay day because past evidence has helped you develop faith that it will just 'be there', the same is expected of you when it comes to your manifestations.

There is no need to continuously hound the company in charge of ensuring your goods get to you because you already know the order is going to be delivered.

One tool I have found priceless when it comes to helping me let go is, of course, meditation.

As we explored in Part 1, all meditation wants is for us is to just 'be'. We usually come to our meditation practice hurried, with our minds bursting full of to-do lists, worries and desires. What meditation actually asks is for you to just allow those thoughts to exist. No judgement, no trying to fix, change or solve. This is the most powerful way to manifest.

And it was through meditation that I came to understand that sometimes the most **well** version of ourselves, might **not** be the living version of ourselves.

Mmmmm hmmmm.

I myself have had to experience what it *really* means to let go.

For those that have read my first book *I Am Not Your Baby Mother*, or engaged with my work as an activist within the Black British birthing space, the next bit will come as no surprise, but for those of you meeting me here, in this phase of my journey, I will quickly bring you up to speed.

In November 2013, I gave birth to my first child. After 26 hours of induced labour that resulted in my dilating to barely two centi-metres, Esmé was born via emergency C-section. The next few days were wrapped in a heady mix of exhaustion and excitement, but I was also feeling desperately unwell. Day by day I felt as if I was being diverted further and further off-course from the healing process.

An abundance of midwives steered me away from my intuition and told me that it was all in my head.

Thankfully, on the fifth night, the source of my illness made itself public. An infection was lingering under my C-section wound, and it had already begun to permeate my bloodstream.

I had sepsis.

I was so unwell I don't remember being rushed back to hospital. To be honest, acceptance was already creeping in. I have since been asked whether it was acceptance or defeat. Allowing myself to be defeated is just not in my nature – I'm a constant kick-back kind of gal – but by this point I was slowly beginning to **accept** that what would be, would be. I was exhausted, not just from childbirth but also from trying to advocate for myself. By the time a stern female surgeon entered my room wondering why I wasn't hastening to 'save my own life', all I could muster was a weak giggle because I found the entire experience so absurd.

'When I'm done speaking to my loved ones, then you can take me down,' I said, through tears.

I'll be honest, I didn't have it in me. There was no desire to fight to stay alive, not even for the sake of my child. I felt my body going supple and relaxing into the next phase. By the time I begun to count backwards and slip out of this consciousness, I was not only ready but also expecting to see my dad.

I had accepted that I wasn't physically strong enough to fight to live.

Sometimes optimum wellness shows up as allowing our bodies to do what they were naturally designed to.

As they wheeled me into that operating theatre, I was shocked at how quickly I had become willing to accept that perhaps the best version of events was one in which I wasn't in physical pain, and was able to support my child from a spiritual plane.

In manifesting terms, it's important to understand that even *after* death we could be used as a tool to kickstart or help support the desires of others.

I have been told that my father wasn't as accepting of his transition. In his last few moments of life, he fought tooth and nail, even kicking a doctor directly in the chest and winding them, such was the vigour with which he tried to cling to this version of life.

There is no sweet way to say this, but I often remark that my dad has been far more useful to me dead than when he was alive. This isn't to say I don't miss him or that often the desire to share something with him doesn't rise up in my chest like a fire and try to suffocate me. But I wouldn't have developed this version of my life, including my understanding of manifestation, if he were still in this life. He has spiritually been most useful to me, and all elements of manifestation, in the next – as an ancestor. We'll cover more about Ancestors in the love pillar, on pages 162–4.

FORGIVENESS

What else might be blocking all your manifestations but particularly your desires connected to wellness?

Our grievances.

Holding on to a grievance can pose a huge threat to our deepest desires and how quickly we can see them come to fruition.

This is because, our main aim is to stay on the highest vibration for as long as possible. We would ideally like to remain there for an eternity, but we are humans facing real-world challenges. It is natural for us to be knocked down a frequency or two from time to time.

With this in mind, let's objectively look at how not being able to forgive can tie us to a vibration that doesn't serve us.

If a grudge were an actual object you could hold, it would be jagged and hot, ready to puncture and burn anything it touches. And this is how not being able to forgive shows up in our lives.

Sticking with my father's death, the emotional hurricane that came with it threatened to decimate me.

My parents came together like Romeo and Juliet, two star-crossed lovers whose paths – let alone their bodies – their families would have preferred never to intertwine. Twenty years after that love was personified through me, and when he died, I felt there was no place for me at his funeral. To this day, I do not know where my father's ashes were scattered, and the only one of his belongings I own is his faded Arsenal mug, which my entire household guards with their lives.

To say I held on to my feelings of exclusion from my father's life would once have been a grave understatement. I actively went out of my way to flood that space with all the negativity I could muster.

I would take any opportunity to head to his house, far out of my way given I didn't live in London anymore. From across the street, I would stare at the home I was raised in, imagining being able to burst through the door and walk into the kitchen where my dad and I would have dance-offs. Or head into the living room and sit on the sofa where we used to watch the 90s morning show *The Big Breakfast*. And, finally, slip into the bed we would share those nights when I would admit I was too scared to sleep alone.

But since none of that was within reach, instead I would hatefully glare at the place, sending out the lowest vibrational energy (hate, anger and destitution). I carried that anger with me, like a cancer, for over a decade.

Until one day I was speaking to a friend who is deeply spiritual. A manifesting maestro who has turned her talents to tarot, she told me that it was time to put my anger to bed.

'I don't want to talk to you the way your dad's spirit is talking to me, as I know what I do is a step too far for you. But you've got to let it go, Kid,' she whispered.

It was the 'Kid' that got me. She could never have known it, but that was his nickname for me. It was always 'Kid' this and 'Kid' that.

'What is coming your way will make whatever you think you're fighting for back here look like rubble. True rubble. He is begging you to let it go. It's this hurt that's standing in between who you are and who you're destined to be.'

121

I thought I was doing a good job of keeping the hate on low heat. Little did I know, I was about to burn the place down. I let my head flop back into the chair I was sitting on, and allowed myself to ugly cry.

Thankfully I was open-minded enough to heed my friend's warning, and slowly, very slowly, I started to work on forgiving those who had caused me so much pain.

In all things I must talk truth, so I'll be the first to admit that this forgiveness has been one of the harder necessities of my life but it **was** a necessity. I couldn't possibly manifest the life I currently have, whilst simultaneously holding on to the hate I had for others, no matter how much I believe they were deserving of it.

I could not possibly manifest my personal version of optimum wellness whilst also holding on to so much hate and anger.

And neither can you. You have to let it go.

So my question to you is:

Who must you work on forgiving?

Whilst only you know the answer to this, I would like to highlight a possible blind spot and point out:

In many cases the first person we must work on forgiving is ourselves.

This has been one of my deepest struggles. There are choices a younger Candice made that have haunted me for years. I won't lie and say that I have not gone to great lengths to understand why that version of myself did this or that. But I will say that every day I work on showing that version of myself grace, because when we know better, we do better.

How do we forgive ourselves?

By using repetition. It's a practice not dissimilar to the Catch it, Kill it, Bin it technique discussed earlier. You have to get into the habit of catching that self-blame and instead extending grace to yourself (or someone else) over and over again. The reason why this isn't a one-and-done scenario is because although many of us would like to, we can't just erase certain memories. There will be times where you are reminded of how poorly another person treated you, or how poorly you treated yourself.

Recently I remarked that if there was any advice I could give to a woman entering their thirties, it would be to not leave the woman they were in their twenties out in the cold. And actually, this is good advice regardless of age. Sometimes it can feel embarrassing to have to recall our past behaviour towards others and ourselves, especially if we were simply in survival mode.

We have to remember that even the choices we made that make us cringe or memories we would rather take to the grave are now part of the make-up of the person who now desires more for themselves. Unfortunately, we might not be able to conceptualise what better could be if we hadn't experienced what we consider to be the worst.

So please, accept that you won't just wake up one day and be wrapped in the soft feeling of forgiveness. Much like many of the new ways of thinking you are engaging with in this book, forgiveness is something that must be exercised every day.

You might add a few lines of self-reflection and forgiveness onto your Good Morning Hygiene routine directly after the Gratitude Greeting. For example:

'I forgive you for those choices you made when you thought you had no other option.'

'I forgive you for not knowing better.'

'I forgive you for not understanding the consequences of your actions.'

There are elements of yourself and your past choices that you need to get into the habit of forgiving. Perhaps you didn't have the knowledge, support network, education or understanding to have made a better choice for yourself. You survived and sometimes that's all we can ask of ourselves.

Most importantly you need to understand that any version of wellness that doesn't want to sit with the idea of forgiveness is not wellness at all. All too often we are encouraged to take shortcuts by acquiring physical things to display as evidence of a life well lived, instead of taking the long route, which is accepting that we have done things we may not be proud of and working through why we did those things. To think you can manifest a higher version of wellness for yourself whilst also holding on to anger and bad vibes is just plain silly. You need to commit to turning that low vibrational energy into something that works *for* you, not against you.

WEALTH

Without a doubt, it is most often money, or more pressingly the lack of it, that pulls people towards the idea of manifestation. Reason being, it's typically the area in which our backs are against the wall. Bills wait for no one. As someone who once had very little money and who now gladly accepts that they are a person worthy of swimming in abundance – not only is my every need met, but there is enough surplus to be able to give freely to others – I'm here to cut through the bullshit.

Money matters.

For me, working with Source to enhance my financial fortitude was something I had to take seriously. I still do. I've written before about watching the electric meter perpetually stuck in E for emergency. Today I am a homeowner with a business that recently turned over seven figures. And I was able to get here in five years.

Wait! Listen! Because I can already hear the creak of the spine as you close this book and grumble 'Cool story, bro, but I don't have five years, the bills are due now!'

As with all of our deepest desires, I can appreciate how much you want to turn your financial status around immediately, but this pillar is going to take work, and time, especially if, like me, you come from a place where the only thing you knew was lack. On the other hand, you also, quite literally, cannot afford to continue thinking the way you always have. Time is going to pass regardless, so why not spend it rewiring your brain to accept the abundance that is already due to you?

First, let's look at your current financial vibration. Perhaps you say things about yourself like:

'I'm so bad with money.'

'I will never be able to afford that!'

'That is way above my pay grade.'

'I can't afford that. Money doesn't grow on trees.'

Perhaps you are physically repulsed by people who present as though they have more than you? Does your internal monologue run something like this?

'They don't deserve that.'

'They are so spoilt.'

'Lucky for some.'

'They have to be doing something dodgy.'

I hate to break it to you, but these thoughts and feelings say so much more about how you feel about yourself than anything to do with others.

And what have I said about the importance of how you **feel**? Exactly.

Your thoughts and words are quite literally priceless. If you don't want to end up becoming a magnet for more lack, your thoughts and words are worth more than any money in your purse. When we repeatedly talk negatively about something we desire or the kind of person we want to be, manifesting these just gets further and further away from us. Look, Source isn't in the business of figuring out how you really feel, it just picks up on what you do and say. So, when it comes to speaking about your own finances or someone who seems very comfortable with theirs, watch your words.

I of all people understand that some people seem to have privileges (usually a word we can preface with white, male and able-bodied) that mean they are on the fast track towards financial ease. This is because the world has wired them to command and, hell, demand more, even if their output is way below their pay grade.

But it is important that you deconstruct why you feel negatively towards people who seemingly make money easily or don't have to struggle. If you don't, you will never manifest to your highest capacity, because how you feel about others is usually an up-to-date map that can guide you towards how you feel about yourself. When I myself decided to do that deep dive, what kept coming up was how undeserving I believed wealthy people to be. But how could I possibly know what they were doing in order to obtain their financial success? When I held the mirror up to myself, it showed the reflection of a woman who actually believed that she herself was undeserving. And don't get me started on this idea that every good thing we see on someone's social media feed is them just 'doing it for the 'gram' – no, sometimes, people are doing very well in real life too. And if you find that off-putting, that is very much a problem that you need to unpack.

In doing so, please understand this:

It is impossible to feel jealousy towards something or someone you don't, in one way or another, admire.

Sure, your first instinct is to allow your ego to kick off and make it about them. But, my dear, jealousy is all about you. And if you read the feeling correctly it can be a very clear marker of what you desire in your own life. If ever you come across a person, place or thing that makes you a little hot under the collar with jealousy, allow yourself to pause and recognise you don't get hot for something you aren't that interested in. And let's be honest, when you don't have much money, seeing someone seemingly enjoying an abundance of it is something that could most definitely bring out the green-eyed monster.

Whilst it may feel that manifesting wealth is somehow different to manifesting your other dreams, I have to emphasise that Source does not see it that way. Humans and their capitalist structures have placed far more importance on, and therefore tension around, money than Source will care to be concerned with. To Source, money is just paper that mortals have put a value on. But for us, due to the value, pressures and expectations we have been taught to associate with it, money seems like the hardest thing to call in. It's not. And that's why the rich seem to get richer. The more money they attract, the more relaxed they become about it. To onlookers it seems as if they don't value money at all. It's not that, they just don't have any resistance towards it, so more flows towards them.

Money is the physical manifestation of an energetic exchange.

I can appreciate that for many that line above might feel like a slap in the face. After all, we live in a world where the cost of living and inflation can mean choosing between filling the fridge or keeping said fridge running. But for those of you still working through your fears around the idea of inviting more in and therefore lessening your magnetism for lack, I have to remind you that we also live in a world where, when it comes to money, your output (how hard you work) no longer determines an employer's input (your wages). The saddest examples of this are, of course, doctors and nurses. We all watched in awe as they risked their lives on the frontline of the Covid pandemic. Although I'm sure the sentiment around standing on our doorsteps and clapping for them was a much-needed morale booster for them, I can guarantee that being compensated as fairly for their time as say, a footballer, would have been a better offering. But interestingly this proves my point: because if we live in a world where effort clearly doesn't correlate to payment, then this also means YOU could be doing less and making more.

So, Candice, you're telling me there is a life I could be living where all my needs and wants are catered for and I don't have to work myself to the bone?

Absolutely. But first, you must believe that there is.

When I began to train my mind to be governed by ideas of abundance instead of lack, my first major hurdle was having to unwire the adage, 'You're going to have to work twice as hard to be half as good.'

For those who share a similar hue to me, this won't be a new saying. Any offspring of an immigrant family will be familiar with this line. Our Ancestors fled their typically warm and vibrant home settings to come and 'succeed' in spaces that were cold and grey in more ways than one. They were greeted by a lack of vitamin D and an abundance of racism that often meant they were forced to disregard the skills they had arrived with and settle for any job they could find. They were forced to play small and remain humble whilst simultaneously working harder than their white peers in exchange for half the compensation or less. As painful as this was it was the only way to survive – fly below the radar and not bring too much attention to themselves. This is a belief that has been passed down.

Yes, we should be grateful for the sacrifices they made. But you are going to have to see their conviction as an idea that has passed its use-by date. Especially if you are going to employ manifestation to create the financial prosperity you desire.

OK, so how?

DEVELOP AN ATTITUDE OF GRATITUDE

'Oh crap! She's on her gratitude bullshit again!'

Firstly, you know I can hear you, right? Secondly, I am! I appreciate that I run the risk of sounding like a broken record – but to be at risk of breaking, you would have already had to play me quite a bit, meaning my message is close to sinking in. So I'll say it again: the quickest way to hack your subconscious is to *feel* good. Now, getting a letter from the debt collectors or hiding in the bathroom from the bailiffs (been there, sweetheart, I was literally late for work waiting for them to leave) doesn't make anyone feel good. It is hard to trick yourself into feeling better about your financial situation when it's just plain shit. So, my only ask is that you start small. The reality is that, even with what feels like nothing, you're better off than many.

It could be that you find the gratitude to have woken up in safe shelter. To have access to clean running water. To perhaps live in a country that will provide help if ever the chips are truly down. True, navigating social care systems can send the sanest person mad, but it's also important to acknowledge that there are services to be accessed in the first place.

Before even trying to ask Source for more, you must show that you are both aware and tremendously grateful for whatever small blessings you already possess.

During this chapter I am going to use the example of homes a lot. I think for me this example works well because, well, homes cost big bucks! Whether renting or buying, the housing market is incredibly swollen and competitive. And, hand on heart, I believe that if I wasn't engaging in the below manifestation practices, there wouldn't be a hope in hell of me acquiring the home of my dreams. For a long while I had to consistently fight against the lie I had heard since I was a teen: 'Just get comfortable in whatever home the council give you, that's as good as you're going to get.'

And it wasn't just what I heard, it's what I saw. Aside from one of my grandparents, everyone I knew and everyone they knew were *enduring* their housing situation instead of *enjoying* it. For many years, I wore that as my truth too. I would never ever have the house of anyone's dreams, let alone my own. So, I started lying to myself, hoping that I would trick myself out of one of my deepest desires:

'I don't even want to own a house anyway. Don't want the headache of the repairs.'

'I like the community aspect of living on this estate.'

'At least the rent is controlled.'

And yet, as I moved from room to room and then flat to flat there was an ever-growing urge to decorate. That urge was actually my true desire slowly coming to the surface. That part of me knew there was power in making every house, no matter how temporary, feel like home. But there was always some pushback to this in the form of unsolicited opinions:

'I don't know why you would bother decorating, it's not even your place.'

'Why would you put this much effort into a home you don't own?'

But I couldn't ignore the call that was begging me to spruce up each place and make it my own. Over time I understood that I was learning to show gratitude towards the place I currently laid my head by beautifying it to the best of my financial ability at the time. In one flat-share it was by laying new carpet in my room, in another house it was by painting the front door. In super small, achievable ways, I was showing gratitude for my current situation.

NOW, GET REAL!

I know, you weren't expecting that, but this step is very important.

For a long time there was one thing I had an abundance of, and it was debt.

Fuck, I even had a debt drawer. Yes, it was a specific drawer where I would shove all my unopened debt-related letters. The reality back then was that no good news was ever coming through my letterbox (I never expected any, and I now understand that this was more than half the problem). So, as soon as a letter came in my name, I would rush to stuff it into this overflowing drawer and make promises that one day, when I won the lottery, I would sort it out.

When I finally decided that enough was enough and I wanted to test what it felt like not to live pay cheque to pay cheque, the first immediate pull I experienced was to 'get real' about my current state of affairs. And looking back, that makes sense. It felt as if Source was asking, 'How can I give you enough to clear these debts, if you don't even know what you need?'

Touché.

And so, heavily pregnant with my son, I pulled the drawer out and let the letters rain down on my bed in a way that I could only hope the dollars would soon be drowning me. Within an hour, once rounded up, I calculated the debt to be close to £10,000.

I let out a sigh, which to my surprise was one of relief. Whilst the debt was about £9,800 more than I currently had to my name, I had also thought it was double, sometimes even triple that. As with most of our fears, they hold no credence when dragged into the light.

Even though at that point I had no idea about how I would clear these debts, I just decided that, because I had made the smallest step towards doing so, a pathway would unfold.

And so that is what I am asking of you. I need you to GET REAL. Be honest about where your finances are currently at. There is no point trying to build a mansion on a cloud. What is more important than the home you're going to build are the foundations of your new financial reality. Because what I can tell you is that, as you develop your money manifestation powers, those foundations will be shaken. Don't worry, they will never collapse, and the slight tremors will always be for good reason: because you will always desire to graduate to the next level. Once you clear your debt, you will want to make more money; then you may want to save for your first home; then you may perhaps want to start a business . . . The reality is, you will never entirely eradicate your worries around lack, or completely hush that whisper that it will all disappear tomorrow (trust me, I've tried), but as you develop a more trusting relation-ship with money and realise how much Source wants to provide for you, you will continue to kick your hopes up a notch. That will, of course, feel scary but like I said, you will shake a little but you will never be stirred! Ha, look at me getting ahead of myself. Let's go back a bit.

I'm gonna need you to . . .

TREAT YA SELF!

Terrible advice, right? *Candice, at this point, you had a second child on the way and two hundred smackers to your name, why would you do that?*

By this stage, I had read enough about manifestation to know that if I wanted change, I had to get busy shifting the atmosphere and one of the quickest ways to do that was to change something in the real world.

And you know what real thing wasn't great? My purse. And that ain't no metaphor, sweetie, I'm talking about my actual purse.

Firstly, it was inherited from someone who didn't allow money to work for them, so I was not off to a great start. I also must acknowledge that the purse was raggedy as hell! It was falling apart at the seams, and the zip would get caught easily, even if it was just on air!

I decided to send a not-so-subtle message to the universe that I was ready for the big bucks by finally treating myself to a new purse. I knew that this would be a good physical way to show that I believed that whatever I spent on the purse would be returned to me, with interest, in due course. And this purse had to be special because, every time I reached for it, whether that was to spend five pounds or five pence, I wanted to send my subconscious the message that I was happy to be doing so, that spending money was a pleasurable experience for me because I had enough of it.

I still have that purse to this day. A deep claret tone etched with an unmistakable logo, I call it my Money Manifestation purse.

Within it is always a couple of pound coins, some American dollars, a citrine crystal (citrine is linked to positivity and is often used to support manifesting the moolah) and, of course, my yearly manifestation cheques (read on for more about these). Whilst the cost of the purse felt like a stretch, it wasn't too far out of my financial comfort zone. And every time I reach for it, I feel rich as hell.

Before I move on to explain what I know is your next question, I really want to emphasise how important it is, where possible, to start investing in yourself in a small, sustainable way. This could be by replacing a tired and empty purse with something more befitting the lifestyle you want for yourself. It could be by getting your nails done, indulging in a hobby once a month or buying yourself a bunch of flowers when surplus funds allow. To be fair, it doesn't matter how you decide to do it, what matters most is the intention behind the action and that it is being done. The call must be coming from inside the house. With what little you currently have, you must show Source that you understand the importance of self-investment because, baby, no one else is going to do this for you. Whilst we are waiting for the big magic to happen, there are small things we can do to help expedite the dream life process, so please don't stand idle in the spaces where you can be making change.

CHEQUE THE TECHNIQUE

Candice, back up a second, who even writes cheques anymore?
Me!

And guess what? I'm only waiting on the universe to cash 'em! But this is a Money Manifestation practice that I can't take credit for. Whilst researching the things I could be doing to help create my dream life, I came across a video by the incredibly talented actor, Jim Carrey. In it he described how he was living in his car, down to his last few dollars, with nothing but some dreams, auditions and a cheque book. He went on to talk about how he decided to pen a cheque to himself with what he believed would be a life-changing sum of money. He signed it and dated it in the future, to the time by which he hoped he would be able to cash the cheque. He made himself a promise that if he wasn't able to cash the cheque by his chosen date, he would pack in acting forever.

Given that we all know who Jim Carrey is by now, I think it should be no surprise that I'm able to announce that this is exactly what happened.

I remember watching the video, then getting up immediately and searching for an old cheque book. In true 'I have no money so I clearly won't be using that' mindset, it seemed that I had thrown mine away. Luckily, Bodé had an old one.

I speedily told him what I needed it for. I was still in the early days of my practices, and he must have thought I had a screw loose. Bless him for not showing it.

That evening, I sat at our rickety kitchen table in the rental home that I felt grateful to afford but truly didn't like that much, let alone love, and allowed my wildest financial dream to flow out of my pen. I wrote out fifteen cheques as if no one was going to tell me 'no'. Not only did I follow Jim's example and date them, I went a step further and signed them from companies that, at that time, I could only dream of working for.

Funnily enough, even though in that moment anyone not on a similar vibration would have accused me of daydreaming or playing pretend, my positive, happy, my-bills-are-paid-my-needs-are-met-all-is-well-and-I'm-forever-abundant energy felt so real that I couldn't help but show all my thirty-two. And like we discussed at the start, **feeling is everything.** A few hours later, when I had to attend to something in my current reality, I allowed that feeling to swallow me whole. Gently I folded up all the cheques and tucked them into my new purse.

'And so it is,' I whispered, softly fingering the leather exterior of my purse, the only place I had ever dared to declare my true financial dreams.

A bit like with Jim, I don't think I need to tell you what happened next. Over the next twelve months, not only did every single cheque clear, more than I was aiming for came to pass. Getting serious about writing my financial desires down was one of the major energy shifters when it came to living a life where the lack of money wasn't at the forefront of my mind.

PLAY MAKE-BELIEVE

Without a doubt, this has to be one of my favourite manifestation tools. And looking back on certain moments in my childhood, I'm not surprised.

When I was in nursery it quickly became clear that the 'home corner' was my favourite, not necessarily because of gender-biased toys like the mini-kitchen or ironing board but because it was home to the dress-up box.

As soon as I arrived, that was the first place I would head and there would always be tears when I was encouraged to play in another area so that other children could have a turn. As I've developed my manifestation skills I have found that 'playing dress-up' allows us to access an energy which, although it might not yet be ours in current reality, is always available for us to try on in the meantime.

And please do not limit this solely to the act of getting dressed (although of course this works too) because I mean this in a much broader sense.

Let's use houses as an example.

Every time I've wanted to move home, I have made it my business to play dress-up in that specific neighbourhood, trying it on for size so to speak.

When making the great escape that was leaving London to head to the shires, my husband and I made more than half a dozen trips to the area we had our eye on. Each time we would 'try on' a different parish, allowing our hearts and minds to acclimatise to the new setting and see if we could visualise ourselves living there long-term. So, this wasn't just about driving around the block once and looking at the properties; we would park up, get out the car and embed ourselves in the landscape for a few hours.

Because this visualisation practice happened at the height of

British summer in a pre-Brexit time, when the sun actually shone for weeks on end, we even made day trips of it. We would pack a picnic, a few blankets and our daughter's scooter and just ... be. There is something tremendously powerful about allowing an atmosphere to wash over you, especially if you are trying to access a new space.

Now to be clear, we weren't in a particularly flush financial situation, but I had worked with Source long enough to know that my sole focus had to be on **feeling** it. After that, the rest would surely follow.

Each time we made a trip, we dialled it up a bit. On some occasions we stopped somewhere to have lunch, on others we visited some of my husband's friends. We essentially made it our business to trick our consciousness into believing this was our usual day-to-day. Once we had grown confident in the task of pretending to live there, we then kicked it up a notch by taking the first baby steps towards making it happen, which for us was viewing properties.

Now, let me admit that this was not entirely smooth sailing and that's because I was a new captain of this Manifestation ship. The reality is I was still at loggerheads with my old patterns, my old way of thinking. Every time we went to view a property that was outside our budget, I felt a little pang of imposter syndrome, like, 'How dare I be tricking this estate agent in this way? How terrible of me!'

I constantly had to remind myself that as a person coming from very little means, this was how 'they' or 'the system' wanted me to feel – as though it were a crime to dream about more for myself. As if it wasn't this estate agent's job to show me around the gaff!

So if you find yourself at mental loggerheads with an old version of yourself, who has grown too comfortable with lack – whether that's because you believe the lie 'more money more problems', or because, as a child, you played small to keep yourself safe and so now reaching for a financial life that offers you more freedom worries you because it will make you more visible – I am here to say that is completely normal.

But I'm also here to say, **'shut up!'** Because if you won't tell that version of you to pipe down, I'm going to have to do it for you. No one knows what you're up to, and to be honest by the time they do, you will be living the life you're pretending to live right now anyway. So, in those moments I need you to get your Viola Davis on, because acting like you already have it means you're very close to that being the truth.

You have to accept that being abundant in any capacity, but especially financially, is going to open you up to scrutiny. Aht aht aht – think about how you spoke about those 'rich folk' – how are you so sure people aren't going to talk the same way about you?

The reality is, you can't be sure. All you can do is work on the fear of being perceived as rich. For many of us, one of the highest hurdles is deep down we worry people will say, 'Oh, she got rich and switched.'

I'm actually laughing out loud as I type because if I had a pound for every time it had circled the block that someone said that about me, I wouldn't need to write this book. I'd be tanning my already black ass on my private island.

Looking back, I was terribly afraid of the gap that would develop between myself and the people I loved who didn't yet love themselves enough to come along with me on this journey. I kept my abundance at bay to keep others comfortable. Don't do what I did.

It was on our final excursion that everything clicked. On the hottest day of the year so far, we were on our way to view a home that I just knew was 'The One'. When we pulled up to its gated front, I allowed myself to believe that we were returning after visiting family in London, not for viewing purposes. As my husband spoke property-speak with the agent, I went from room to room, mentally assigning each one their use, and envisioning where all our current furniture would go. When we left, we decided to really take in the local neighbourhood before heading back to the city. We found ourselves on the cobbled road that was the local high street. Perhaps it was because there wasn't a cloud in the sky, bunting was up and everyone was basking in the joy that comes along with summer, but it was breathtaking. As a final nod to what a fairy tale this place could be, there was an old-fashioned ice-cream stand, which we decided to stop at to cool ourselves down.

'Man, I could get used to this,' my husband sighed, before quickly taking a lick from my ice cream. On any other day that would have pissed me off, but there was just no room for negativity here.

'I already have!' I shot back.

'Me too!' Esmé squealed.

I think it's safe to say, we were all in agreement about the vibration we were emitting in that moment.

A few hours later as we approached home, we got a call to say that the landlord had accepted our offer. And I can't lie and say I was surprised, because how was it going to go any other way?

I have since deployed these tactics multiple times when we've come to moving home. When we had outgrown our last home and we decided to try and get on the property ladder, I decided to kick it up a notch.

DEAR FUTURE YOU

Unlike most who make a foolproof, airtight, unicorn-blessed plan when deciding to buy their first property, ours kind of happened by mistake.

'Can you give the mortgage broker a call and see what we will have to do in order to purchase a property in the next three years?' I asked Bodé one day.

'Sure!' he said trying and failing to mask the shock and slight excitement in his tone.

I hid my smirk. Yes, the tide had turned. When we first started dating, I sporadically made it crystal clear just how unfeasible I thought getting on the property ladder was for us. I didn't have the resources or the generational wealth that was seemingly required to buy a bag of bricks, let alone a full-blown house. I had secretly signed off on being an eternal renter. But between clearing my debt, doubling my income and having a landlord who lived in the house next door who thought he could drop in whenever he wanted, I knew the time was right to start stirring the cauldron. I mean, all I wanted to do was *see* what we would have to do in order to make this happen in the future. No big deal.

A few hours later, it was as if I lived in a snow globe that had been turned upside-down.

'OK, make this clear to me,' I begged Bodé, as my heart began to race. 'What do you mean he said we're good to go now?' I asked disbelievingly.

Bodé sighed, clearly exasperated by having to explain for a third time. 'Babe, they've run the numbers. As long as we can come up with the deposit, we could be out of here within the year,' he confirmed again.

We sat at the kitchen table so Bodé could explain things in depth. We were first-time buyers, so because of the government's Help to Buy scheme at that time, we would pay 0% Stamp Duty on our purchase. The deposit wasn't that far out of reach, thanks to the savings we had been able to accumulate over time.

This was music to my ears. To be honest the house that had been perfect whilst I was pregnant was now slowly shrinking. Between the boiler that was over twenty years old, which our landlord refused to replace because he still knew of the one shop where he could procure parts, and the invasion of gargantuan spiders that happened like clockwork between September and December, I was responding to an atmosphere that was no longer allowing me to live my best life. That week alone, the boiler had failed three times and I'd almost lost my now almost one-year-old son RJ to the nearby A-road when an arachnid that looked like one more commonly found in the Australian outback had made an appearance on the hood of his buggy. If manifestation had taught me one thing, it was to **pay attention to when an environment felt unfavourable**. From housing to work, if time spent in a space gives you more anxiety than respite, get busy manifesting a way out.

'Well shiiiiiit,' I sighed in my best Katt Williams voice.

The next few weeks went by in a blur. All of a sudden, strangers required every piece of paperwork I'd ever generated since being born; the intrusion into our finances reaching fever pitch when I was questioned about the cost of my twice monthly therapy sessions. But, inch by inch, we were moving towards a new reality.

After looking at multiple properties, we stumbled across a four-bed in a new parish less than a mile from where we were currently situated. It was the only home available for now, and we decided to just go for it, paying the small fee to have it taken off the market.

While our mortgage broker was decidedly positive, he did remind us that there were always some kinks in the process that could mean that the house could still potentially be sold to someone else.

I was already so invested in getting out of my Little Miss Muffet situation that I knew I had to add something else to my manifestation arsenal – and that's where letter writing came in.

Letter writing, especially by hand, now feels so quaint, like a vintage pastime. But putting pen in hand and setting our hopes down on paper is still one of the most powerful ways to bring our manifestations to fruition.

THE 'SCIENCE'

Writing by hand fires up the parts of your brain that deal with your thinking and your long-and short-term memory, allowing you to store and manage information. The strokes made by the pen and your hand can help you encode whatever you are scripting, ensuring that what you are writing really sticks in your mind.

And so that's exactly what I got busy doing. But unlike previous instances, where I kept the letters to myself, I knew there was a little more I could do to make this house our home. I decided to purchase a card that had 'Congratulations on Your New Home' inscribed in gold foil font above a cute illustration of a cottage. In that card, I wrote to my future self, telling her how proud I was of her for accepting that she was worthy of this desire. I told her that she should look on this as a lesson on what can be accomplished when she had the courage to take a leap and bet on herself. I finished by wishing her great health and happiness for the rest of her days. And yes, then I did what any 'crazy' person would do. I walked to the house and put the letter through the door, secure in the knowledge that the person who would open that letter was myself.

To up the ante on the magic even more, I had friends and family follow suit. Luckily they were all hip to my 'woo woo' ways by now, so it took (almost) no cajoling at all.

And you know what? By the time we collected the keys and opened the door, there were ten or so welcome cards waiting for me to open.

So even though you may not have done it since you a had a penpal (remember those?) if you are physically able, I really encourage you to get to grips with letter writing once more. And please remember letter writing need not be only for you to talk about your financial desires, these letters could be congratulating you for anything relating to any pillar.

THE PRACTICE: **LETTER WRITING**

The key with letter writing for manifestation is to scribe as though the magic has already happened. Whilst you will, of course, be writing to *future* you, achieving your desires **should all be penned in the past tense**, as though the deal has already been done. For example:

Dear Symone,
I hope you're well. It's been so incredible to watch you settle into your new job role as HR manager.

To my darling Cynthia,
I still can't quite believe how incredible it must have felt to finally achieve the marathon time that you worked so hard for.

Dearest Temi,
I know it wasn't always easy, but look at how well you have adjusted to your new, wonderful life after divorcing that asshole!

I think you get my point.

I encourage you to really let loose with your projections here. Perhaps it's the writer in me, but I want you to fully use your imagination and allow your desires to have no limits. You will know when you've gone as far as you can, because you will start to feel a little nervous, almost a bit cheeky. There will be a part of your brain yelling, 'who do you think you are?!' but don't let that put you off. This is your time to really speak to the version of you who has already achieved everything you can think of.

Whilst I prefer to manifest solo, I have friends who host letter writing gatherings. It can be a very powerful group exercise. I mean just imagine the how high the vibration is in a space filled with people who are getting busy feeling excited about their future? Something tells me it must feel magical. And like I did with the cards being sent to my home, feel free to rope your family and friends into this too – just make sure they want the best for you (more on that in the love pillar).

GET GOOD AT GIVING

When you find your financial sphere beginning to expand, it is important that you invite others into the circle of abundance by becoming a giver.

Giving benefits the recipient, but the secondary effect of giving – its effect on the giver – is even more powerful. Giving signifies that there is no fear of loss and that you believe anything given will be returned to you. We have to keep reminding ourselves that **money is just a physical representation of energy exchange** (see page 129). The more flexible you become with what you have, the quicker Source will realise that you see money for what it really is and present you with more opportunities to be a giver.

Now be warned that for many of us, money can also be attached to trauma, which can be triggered when we least expect it.

When I first found myself floating down the river of abundance, I thought it was my true duty to try and be charitable to everyone I met. I even included those who had made it crystal clear that they didn't like bus-taking Candice at all, and they were only now putting up with me because there was space in my new limo.

The issue was that money seemingly bought me the one thing I had struggled with my whole life, which was simply not only to be accepted, but also be liked.

In one instance I treated someone to a wonderful holiday, during which I covered every expense and even purchased them beautiful jewellery. Shockingly, one night, when they thought I was asleep, I overheard them on the phone verbally decimating me to one of their friends. I was called every name under the sun, with no mention of all the generosity they had experienced.

With tears blurring my sight, I cried myself to sleep, promising myself that the second my feet touched British soil, I would not only put a hard stop on that relationship, but would also take a long hard look at why I desired to buy this person's attention, care and love so much.

As with all things mentioned in this book, it is important to keep your intuition front and centre. Take a look at why you're giving and where the urge comes from. Don't let your desire to be *seen giving* trump the reason *why* you're giving. In fact, the best way to test this is, before you give is to ask yourself, 'if no one were to ever know about my good deed other than the recipient, how would that make me feel?' Our initial answer is usually a good marker of whether we should proceed or not. And listen, I'm human, so there are still plenty of times that, when I check myself, I have to admit that I'm about to give not for that personal warm and fuzzy feeling but for public praise. No matter how much money you manifest, you cannot buy your way into people's good graces. You must let people build whatever false narrative they use to entertain themselves without trying to use the act of giving to change their minds. Here's what I have learned:

There will be no spiritual repercussions if you do not give to someone who disrespects you.

There will be no curse of lack if you stop giving to someone when you realise they see you as nothing but a cash cow.

There will be no financial or spiritual retribution if you feel as though continuing to give is going to land you back in a financial situation that you have physically and spiritually worked hard to leave in the past.

I have decided to put the above in bold as it is very important that we don't allow guilt or pressure to turn what could be an all-round feel-good act into something that feels like an unwanted responsibility.

As with all manifestations the root of it all lies in the intention. If you are giving from a negative place, the only return on that can be negative. But if you are in a place to give with a willing heart, then always do so because the energetic messaging will always be positive.

MONEY ~~TALKS~~ LISTENS

As ever, when trying to manifest a new material world for yourself, it is very important to watch your mouth, because money always listens.

Whilst of course it doesn't have a physical set of ears, the energy of money always has one metaphorical ear to the door and, as we covered on page 127, if money overhears you berating it, saying how much stress it brings to your life then it will in fact keep the hell away from you.

When did you ever want to keep up with a friend who you knew good and well was chatting shit about you? Exactly.

You want to talk about money as if it were your best friend, as if it provides security and comfort. As if it's a tool that is going to help you live a life **filled with more ease and less resistance.**

Let's look at some of the ways we could be keeping money at bay with the things we say:

'All rich people are crooks.'

'Money is the root of all evil.'

'Money stresses me out.'

'I wouldn't know what to do with all of that money.'

'I barely have enough money to pay these bills.'

'Money is the root of all my stresses.'

I could perhaps fill the rest of the book with language like this, but I think you get the picture.

Now let's brainstorm some of the ways we could be talking about money even if we are waiting for it to manifest in the physical.

'Money is a tool that will make this element of my life easier.'

'I can't wait to be able to share my wealth.'

'I'm so grateful that I was able to cover [insert debt payment] this month. I'm excited for when I'm able to pay off even more.'

'More money will allow me the headspace to be more creative and worry less.'

The more positively you speak about money even in your pathway to growing into abundance, the more money will physically respond.

Funnily enough, as I was writing this chapter, the most powerful example manifested itself.

I was in the first-class lounge at an airport waiting to board a flight to somewhere with high temperatures and cocktails on tap.

With one ear trained on my kids, I used to other to soak up the conversations around me.

Directly behind me were a family of five. From the conversation I gathered they had never been in a first-class lounge before.

'I wouldn't pay excess for this shit. Might as well just eat at McDonald's,' said a male voice.

'I know! I don't get this, I think it's all so unnecessary,' responded the mother figure.

'Well, I think it's quite cool. It's nice to have somewhere to relax and not queue for food,' said a younger, male voice.

I felt a small smile spread across my face.

'Well, you're the same lad who spent forty quid on a *inaudible*, so of course this doesn't seem excessive to you. You're not made of money, kid, don't forget it,' shot back the first male voice.

I felt my smile crumble and my blood grow hot. It took all I had within me to not turn around and let the young lad know that it was important that he didn't let anyone break his abundant spirit, that whenever he could, he should allow himself to bathe in whatever he deemed luxury, as it was only through doing so that he could widen his net of abundance. But of course I kept my head straight, annoyed at what I had just heard.

Less than a few minutes a later the complete opposite happened.

'Sorry ma'am, have you been here before?' asked a tanned, dark-haired man as I juggled my coffee and free pastries.

'Uh, yeah,' I responded.

'Oh! I was just going to let you know they even have showers! It's my first time, see!'

I felt a wide smile develop in response to how happy he was.

'If I had known that, I wouldn't have gotten up at the crack of dawn to shower! This is so cool!' he laughed.

'Isn't it?!' I giggled.

'Yeah, I'm going to try and make this happen again. This is the life!' he concluded before swiping a croissant and bopping away, leaving behind what felt like nothing but sunshine, glitter and rainbows.

I felt happier at having witnessed his happiness.

I returned to my seat knowing for sure that he would experience this again and again and again, because his energy said so.

And I couldn't help but notice that, because I was now writing about money and our energy towards it, Source had very quickly presented me with two polarising examples. It was as if it wanted to remind me, and you the reader, how money is always listening, not just to how you feel about it, but most importantly, how you feel about yourself.

DOUBLE T-APP

Now this last little secret is particularly rogue, but it has been so transformative to my financial vibrations that I couldn't help but share. It's a money app.

Yep, an app, called The Secret to Money.

Quite simply, twice a day this app on my phone sends me an imaginary £250,000, and every day it asks me to list what I would like to spend the money on. At first, the question felt very over-whelming and mirrored my real-life feelings around money. I wouldn't even spend the entirety of the imaginary cheque every day, as I was fearful that there would not be any money left over. As time has gone on, I have come to expect the thrill of the ker-ching the app makes as it delivers my cash every day. Now I spend my metaphor-ical cheque with glee, knowing that, like clockwork, more will be available to me tomorrow.

It's been scientifically proven how bad certain apps can be for us and how they negatively work their way into our psyche, but what about the reverse? What if there was technology that helped us reframe our attitudes, leading to a more positive experience?

Another great thing about this app is that it prompts me to list the money I have accrued that day in real life. Outside of budgeting and bill-paying, sometimes it's easy to forget the positives involved with money-making. When I can remember to, nothing gives me a greater thrill than to write out how much income is coming my way. To date, that section of the app sits at £1.6 million, and that is with me not being diligent about recording every pound that comes my way. Even so, it bears testament to the fact that the pounds are indeed coming in abundantly.

To conclude, although I've shared with you how I changed and continue to enlarge my financial landscape, I must reiterate two things. Firstly, none of these practices is a one-and-done. As with all things that improve us, discipline and consistency are the true game-changers. My Money Manifestation practices now vary based on the level of support I need at the time. And, as with all the advice

I offer in this book, it's important that you listen to your intuition with regard to what tools you may need to use at any given time. The second thing is that, even though I am confident in my Money Manifestation capabilities, there are still times where fear or doubt creeps back in. This is completely normal. In fact, there are times where I find these little shakes in faith very necessary as, more often than not, these cracks have appeared because I have not been consistent enough in the practices that keep my foundation solid. So, if you find yourself feeling fear over lack, or notice old worries creeping back in about returning to a time when you financially struggled, know that you aren't alone. But don't let it sully all your hard work so far. This is simply a reminder to get back on 'your zoom' (as the young folk say) and raise what I know you to be, which is a very powerful money maker.

 **LOVE**

As kismet would have it, I have come to write this chapter on my wedding anniversary, so thankfully I am very much in the mood to not only to talk about love but most importantly, about how you can manifest it.

Of all the pillars, this is of course the one we need the most. At the time I am writing this, there is a very public genocide happening, which is rooted in our inability to love one another regardless of differences. Whilst this turmoil feels physically far removed from me and my day-to-day life, energetically its ricochets and aftershocks are as powerful as any missile.

With social media now being a wide window into so many other ways of life but most importantly our humanity, I can say without doubt that love is lacking in every fragment of our universe.

Because only lovelessness could be the reason we seek to bring pain, destruction and terror to our fellow human beings.

Our current global vibration isn't just low, it's on the floor.

Forever being the optimist I am, I maintain that this doesn't mean all is lost. It's the sporadic acts of love on big and small scales that will keep us all going.

I can appreciate that romantic love and how to manifest it may be your primary concern. And there is nothing wrong with that, I would even argue that if it were not, then I would worry slightly. To admit that to love and be loved is a goal is, of course, the first step to getting what you desire. But it is important to recognise that romantic love isn't the only kind worth manifesting, and the other versions of love are just as instrumental to manifesting your dream significant other (more on that later).

As ever, let's start with self.

SELF-LOVE

My first question is:

Do you love yourself?

Notice I didn't ask do you like, accept or feel good about yourself. I specifically asked about love. And the thing with self-love is that, for it to be in its purest form, it has to be unconditional.

You cannot only love yourself when you're dolled up; you must also love yourself in a mismatched tracksuit or with your bonnet on. You cannot only love yourself when you feel you are accomplishing milestones in your chosen career; you must also love yourself when goals aren't being met.

So now I've put it like that, you might find that no, you don't love yourself quite yet. And that's fine, so long as there is a commitment to getting there because – and I'm sure you've heard this before – to dive headfirst into manifesting romantic love without first conquering the divine task of loving oneself, is for sure the true definition of putting the cart before the horse.

So, Candice, how do I love myself?

Before you ask me that question, let me say that now would be a great time to use an ASKfirmation. Make a note to do this, as I want you to encourage your brain to answer this question on your own behalf. But in the meantime, I will say that loving oneself must start with self-acceptance.

This can be the hardest attribute to master, especially if you were raised in a family, household or community who *tolerated* you, but didn't truly *accept* you. So much of our inability to develop self-love is often rooted in not being encouraged or given the space to love ourselves in our formative years.

As the first-born female in a Caribbean household, I know that what I'm about to break down is not unique to me.

I found that as I approached my pre-teen years, the words used to describe me became diminishing and cutting. I was told in a plethora of ways how not quite 'up to par' I was.

This 'death by a thousand cuts' could range from female family members frequently telling me how my body type wasn't loveable, to strangers making it clear that even if I were of age to be romantically involved with them, they would go out of their way not to be with me.

These unwanted opinions felt more jagged due to them being

presented against a backdrop of a society who never missed a beat when it came to telling me how unworthy I was, simply by never representing me.

For many of you reading this, you may struggle with self-love because there was no safe space to develop it. There were no adults telling you that you were in fact enough. You did not see yourself represented as a loveable being in mainstream media.

For people like you, *people like us*, we are going to have to go back to the start and rebuild a foundation of self-love first and foremost.

One practical and quick way to do this is to **create a self-gratifying echo chamber.**

Often we are told that echo chambers are bad things, as they limit our ability to hear from all different walks of life. But what I am going to need you to do when it comes to manifesting self-love is to work at creating a space where you are upheld as the most beloved being. Obviously, the wider world is out of the question. Whilst some suggest that the most marginalised should continue to fight to be seen and respected and finally loved, as a marginalised woman myself, I say politely that those well-meaning folk can all do one.

Continuously fighting to be seen as worthy can be too much of a task for so many of us. It is exhausting to have to continuously prove your value. It is my true belief that this time is far better spent creating and curating spaces in which you are number one.

The easiest way to do this is digitally.

Make sure the social media platforms you use are full to the brim of positive reflections of yourself.

Of course, this isn't to say not to follow people who don't resemble you, but it is a reminder that you have the power to create a space in which your likeness is the majority of what you see especially if, in the physical world, you aren't part of that club.

My next question is:

How do you treat people that look like you?

Whilst it may feel like a silly ask at first, let's sit with it for a moment.

For transparency, I spent years treating women who looked like me quite poorly. The root of this behaviour was internalised misogynoir combined with a fear that I had to treat them badly before they could do the same to me. I took the poor treatment offered up by others and sought to quickly deliver it to people who looked like me, like a hurtful game of pass-the-parcel. When we don't yet truly love ourselves, it can be far too easy to be hateful towards those who look like us. And this behaviour needs to be checked, as it is of very low vibrational quality.

There is also something to be said for how this shows up in minority communities. Slavery and colonisation have done a superb job at making Black people fear their own. As an example, this is reflected in the rhetoric around police brutality. Amongst comment sections densely populated with Black people it's not unusual to find those who will try to justify what is happening to one of their own:

'Oh well, if only he wasn't wearing a hoodie.'

'She should've known better than to talk to the policeman like that.'

'See, there we go making a fuss again.'

What is happening there is a projection of self-hate. A falsehood that, if only this person were a 'good Black', like they believe themselves to be, this wouldn't happen. Of course, nothing could be further from the truth. No amount of codeswitching or cosplaying is going to make the difference to life of a Black person who unfortunately runs into a white police officer who was just 'having a bad day'.

One way to manifest self-love is to adorn those who look like you with the kindness, support and empathy you wish to receive.

THE ANCESTORS

Let's pause here for a minute, and think about those who may have looked like us, but who lived before we were born.

On the face of it, ancestors are simply the people we descend from – we all have them. But many Black people have Ancestors with a capital A.

Reverence for, and belief in Ancestors can be found all over the world. In China there is the Holy Ghost festival, in Cambodia there is Pchum Ben, and of course we cannot forget the more commonly known El Día De Los Muertos, 'The Day of the Dead', in Mexico.

But I don't want to blanket this Ancestral experience, so I'm now strictly speaking as me, Candice Brathwaite. For me, the Ancestors are family members who have passed on but who, even in their spiritual form, are committed to the protection and betterment of their lineage and who, in my physical form, I respect and uphold for the sacrifices they made and any help they decide to give.

Just as I wish to make headway on rocky terrain so that my off-spring need not face the same difficulties, I like to think that this is exactly what my Ancestors intended when they made their gargan-tuan, difficult life choices. I think many of them knew they would more than likely not be the beneficiary of the risks they took, but they decided it was worth it regardless. They did it for us.

To be clear, your Ancestors need not be someone you met when they were alive. Some of my favourite Ancestors are relatives I have heard many a wonderful story about, or those I have been able to research. But while you do not need to have known some-one personally when they were alive, you do need to be clear about the kind of ancestors you would like to support you. Not every family member is worthy of being an Ancestor, for instance. As in all things, we must be guided be our intuition. In some areas of your life, it could be particularly helpful to call on an ancestor with a loving paternal spirit and in other instances, you are going to have to call on one who knows how to fight. Of course, they can't come and throw hands for you in the physical, but you can trust they are going to deploy all their spiritual power to ensure that those who try to mess with you just get the message that you ain't the one.

But where do the Ancestors fit into manifesting love?

By us connecting with them. People choose to do this in a variety of ways but the most popular way amongst my living loved ones is to have an Ancestral Altar. It's not nearly as half as elaborate or difficult as it sounds – it can simply be a window ledge or table where we keep their photos, things they owned or talismans that remind us of them.

In many cultures it is very normal to 'greet' the Ancestors each morning and also give them a 'offering'. Offerings can come in many forms, with the most popular being food, lighting candles and sometimes even money. The offering is all about showing gratitude towards them and all the work they undertook for you to be currently where you are.

Honouring your ancestors can help provide clarity in times of difficulty, but it is also a way in which you can gain strength. It is very comforting to know that no matter what you are facing in this moment, someone from your bloodline has more than likely had to face a similar and more often than not, harder trial.

When it comes to manifesting, I often ask for the guidance of my Ancestors when it comes to protection and decision-making. It is thought that the Ancestors have a clearer view of what or who could be sending us low vibrational energy. I usually use gratitude and meditation (see Part 1 for more on this) in order to help me connect with them. But I must warn you, when you start to do this work you may not always like the answers you receive.

It was one of my Ancestors who let me know that, by not showing self-love through my friendships, I was causing the biggest barrier between who I currently was and who I wanted to be (see pages 185–6).

DATE YOURSELF

Another way to instigate self-love is to date yourself.

The primary way to date yourself is to send time **alone** with yourself doing things that bring you joy.

There are many people miserably waiting for their 'better' half to come along before they begin dating. The problem with that is, most of the time, dating is encumbered by elements of desiring to impress someone, in the hope that they will endeavour to develop something more serious with you.

Dating yourself is low risk and absolutely vital to understanding what sparks your self-love. As someone who has been in a relationship with their significant other for a long time, I still make it a priority to date myself.

At least once a month I schedule a 'me' day in my calendar. I will usually use this day to go to an art gallery or to the cinema. Both are activities that feel as though they can be more impactful done solo, as the focus is on internal dialogue. Looking at or watching a piece of art allows me to formulate a conversation with myself. There is no need to feel as though I am performing. I can simply be.

Much like in my romantic relationship, my relationship with myself is always changing. I owe it to the most important version of myself to stay in tune with what sets her alight.

These dates need not be extravagant or give you the ick. If you aren't yet comfortable with going to a restaurant by yourself, how about you take yourself to the park, or out for coffee? The task here is to really revel in your own company and get comfortable with being the master of your own destiny.

REPROGRAMME YOUR SELF-LOVE SUBCONSCIOUS

Remember how I said that this is the perfect time to use ASKfirmations? And remember how on pages 63–5 I mentioned how powerful it is to put pen to paper? Well, now would be a good time for you to do both those things.

Using Post-it notes, I want you to hand write some ASKfirmations that inspire answers about your self-love.

Here are three questions you can start with:

'Why am I so wonderful to spend time with?'

'How come I feel so comfortable with myself?'

'What could I do today to fall more in love with myself?'

These questions are just a starting point; I encourage you to go to town. You only need to write the question down. Reason being, we don't want a concrete answer that then limits our ability to find out even more magical things about ourselves. Give your brain the space to always come up with new answers. This exercise should take no more than an hour. When you're done, I want you to stick these Post-it note questions on the mirrors you use the most. It is very important that you are confronted by your own beautiful reflection when working with these ASKfirmations.

As with all the advice I've given in this manual thus far, these elements must be habitual. This is not a one-and-done situation. This is a daily commitment to rewiring our subconscious and accepting and then expecting all our wildest desires to materialise.

Present you has to believe that future you is worth the effort.

Now, let's think about what we could do to help bring someone else into the fold.

ROMANTIC LOVE

Before you even ask, no you cannot manifest a romantic relationship with one specific person. Not unless they too are drawn to you in that way.

To try and manifest another person is to try to intercept their free will and essentially play God. I must briefly say that manifestation is not witchcraft or 'black magic'. We want to learn to work with what is already present within ourselves to help produce the positive energy necessary to extract our deepest desires and make them a reality. What I have no interest or practice in is casting a spell over another human in the hope that they will fall in love.

But Candice, how can I manifest the person of my dreams?

Easy peasy, sweetheart, if you remember that it's all energy. As we explored in the money pillar, love is another aspect of life that, thanks to how society has conditioned us, we believe to be hard to find. To *find*, yes. Because in this manifestation game of cat and mouse, the more desperate you are for something, the more it will camouflage itself.

The energy of 'looking' is read by the universe as 'lacking'; it cannot decode it any other way. We don't look for something we believe is already ours, we simply enjoy it. The more you *search* for the person of your dreams the harder they will be to find because you are simply maximising the energy of desperation not completion.

Ha! Let me not lie, like everything this pillar is going to require work, patience and discipline.

But, of course, you can manifest the love of your dreams. Whilst I've already warned you about trying to manifest a particular person, you can manifest someone whose personality and attributes make your heart flutter.

If it is meant to be, working on attracting someone like that into your life could mean it is someone specific that answers the call. But the reason I harp on about not homing in on one particular person is because in this digital age, you perhaps don't know them as well as Source does.

If you think you are in love with someone you see online or spend limited time with, the reality is that you aren't. You don't *really* know them. What has happened is that you are infatuated with who you *think* they are, **not** who they really are.

IT'S WORTH THE WAIT

When trying to manifest your dream person, it is important to not waste energy on someone who is clearly a placeholder.

Passive dating as a way to pass the time is still using energy that could be better spent in the tank of self-love rather than 'OK for now love'. Spending time with people who, deep down, we know we are simply 'settling' for is the quickest way to slow down bringing in who we truly want.

Remember, Source wants clear and consistent direction. Cultivating a manifestation full to the brim of the attributes of your dream person only to then go out on countless dates with people who have none of the character traits you are looking for in a significant other is a slap in the face to both you and Source.

Stop wasting your time.

Stop wasting their time.

Stop confusing Source.

As someone often paralysed by social anxiety, I can appreciate that what I'm about to say next may scare many of you.

You are not going to meet your dream person at home.

When working to manifest our significant other we must take the energy, well, outside! Where you choose to go is up to you, but my advice would be to frequent places connected to those you already enjoy. If you would like someone to share your interest in art, then I would say circling the golf course isn't the best use of your time.

Now note that I said, 'places you enjoy' not 'places where you think you will find someone'.

Speaking from the perspective of a heterosexual woman I must admit I have seen too many wonderful women fall at the first hurdle by prematurely contorting themselves into what they believe their future other half may desire them to be, instead of standing firm in who they are and what their desires are.

This is a huge error, as should a relationship develop at the lowest end of the scale, resentment will develop. At the opposite end it just screams, 'divorce!' as you have hidden parts of yourself that cannot stay locked away for an eternity.

BECOME SELF-OBSESSED

In perhaps the riskiest advice ever given when it comes to manifesting romantic love, I am going to demand that you become self-obsessed. This is a two-pronged approach. Firstly, it centres *you* as the most important character in your love story. Secondly, it sends a message to Source that you trust the energy enough to deliver your significant other when the time is right. So, you can spend this time being absolutely obsessed with yourself.

I want you to be so high off your own supply that it truly is going to take someone special for you to turn your head. And whilst it may be an unconventional requirement, I am living proof that this works.

When I met my now husband, I was many chapters into the most self-obsessed era of my life. A painfully pathetic almost two-year relationship had finally drawn to a close and in true rom-com fashion, I had drunkenly wept all over my girlfriends, telling them that I was done with this dating malarkey.

I dramatically announced that I needed to spend time with myself and work on rebuilding some of the key elements of self-love that had been blown into oblivion by trying to be what I thought my ex desired, instead of being clear about what I wanted to be.

And whilst admittedly there were a few hiccups along the way, I was intentional about living the best life I could without feeling that I needed a person to complete me. I recommitted to my health and fitness journey and spent most of my free time delighting in activities that set me alight like travel, running and socialising with friends.

When it came to thinking about another person, although I assumed I wasn't giving it much thought, in retrospect my subconscious was getting busy. This messaging worked because I was crystal clear about what I *did not* want.

Looking back, I have to admit that this phase was the quietest of all my dating life and it was simply because, without knowing it, I was putting up invisible blockers to bullshit. So let me forewarn you, as you develop this skill your phone is going to stop ringing – and that's how we know the manifestation is working, because the line needs to remain open for the right person to call.

What being self-obsessed taught me was (you've heard it before):
You don't get what you ask for, you get what you are.

I wasn't physically asking for anything at all. But what I was doing was doubling down on how well I treated myself and respected my boundaries and this simply became who I *was*, as a person. I felt good about myself and about being with myself most of the time.

You cannot manifest the person of your dreams whilst feeling like shit. You must first feel good to then attract the goodness that comes from being intimate with someone you desire.

I was no longer willing to modify or contort myself in order to catch the eye of some suitor. It had to be all or nothing, with me as the ultimate prize. I was in my own world, so much so that I was borderline deluded.

And then like a comet crossing the night sky, someone popped up with all of the attributes I desired.

I mean, it felt cosmic, electric.

Like something that could only be the outcome of big magic.

Bodé and I fell hard and fast. Within a month we were living together, and aside from (much needed) solo holidays, we haven't been apart for the past twelve years.

But the gag is, I wasn't looking for this dude! I was looking for myself with the deep faith that when the time was right, I would be met with a person I didn't have to negotiate with nor rework myself for.

I guess now is a great time to admit that if I had been consciously trying to manifest my husband at that time, then I would have perhaps ended up with someone who physically looks very different.

Physical attraction is extremely important but sometimes we can get so hard-headed about a particular weight, height, skin tone and eye colour that we can completely ice out what could be the exact match for our heart's desires.

When it comes to manifesting romantic love, we cannot get too hung up on the packaging if the content is hitting it out the park. To be clear, I'm not asking you to force nor ignore your sexual desire, but I am asking you to be open to the multitude of ways you can be disarmed by big love.

If you are being extremely rigid about your potential person's physical attributes you must understand that this is energetically limiting the mind-blowing connection that is waiting for you.

Allow Source to be limitless in the multitude of ways big love can be presented to you.

Have you ever connected with someone whom on paper, you swore you couldn't possibly be attracted to? You know, those instances where eye contact was held for far longer than was necessary? Where there was a desire to be closer to them even in an already small room? That invisible pull to wanting to know so much about them it's as if time evaporates whenever they talk? And yet they're not your 'type'?

Yeah, there could be something there. It would be a true shame if you let your preconceived ideas, or worse still what society dictates you should find attractive, put this fire out.

GO WHERE THE LOVE IS

Now, when we're talking about the manifestation of romantic love, nothing could be more powerful than having an orgasm.

Candice, I done told you I haven't met them yet.

Hush, hush, I know.

It's a shame, especially for women, that when we think about orgasms it is often not outside of the pleasure we can offer. What I'm about to talk about is exclusively tied to self-pleasure and self-love.

Using masturbation when trying to manifest romantic love has to be one of the oldest tricks in the book.

There is no energy more powerful, precise or intentional than sexual energy. Simply put, it is the force that keeps the human race going. If you've ever experienced an orgasm so earth-shattering that it was as if you heard colour and were able to see sound, then you know exactly what I'm talking about.

I know for some reading this that using orgasmic energy as a way to manifest will be a step too far and of course that's fine – but let me at least try and soften you with the facts.

THE 'SCIENCE': **ORGASMS**

Sex creates life. Every single atom that fuses together to make you you, was created through sex. If you ever need evidence to support how powerful manifestation is, put your hand to your chest and feel your heartbeat. It is highly likely that you are the physical manifestation of someone's energetic desire. Is there anything more powerful than that?

Using the clarity of mind and powerful sexual energy that happens when we orgasm is not dissimilar to tantric sex, which dates back more than six thousand years. As with tantric sex, by using orgasms to manifest we are trying to marry the spiritual and the physical. You are more than welcome to work on tantric sex once you've manifested your dream sexual partner but in the process of doing so, don't shy away from the power that private pleasure holds.

For many of you, I understand how self-pleasure in this way is going to take courage, as you perhaps come from a space where you were incorrectly taught to feel shame about your body. You may even have been conditioned to believe that your sexual energy should solely be for the use of others. Even thinking about doing anything other than that is a sin in some cultures.

If you feel deeply opposed to this way of manifesting, I would encourage you to spend time with yourself or a therapist exploring why, as the root of your reasoning could perhaps go on to show up as blocks in other areas of your manifestation journey, and I wouldn't want that for you.

I must say that my ever-evolving experience with using sex and self-pleasure to manifest has been a jaw-droppingly exciting experience. Don't just think that you should use this practice to help manifest someone to share the bed with; this practice can be used for all of your desires. I have used this practice to manifest homes, contracts and money. When working with desire, no dream is off limits.

THE PRACTICE: **ORGASMS**

When spending time with yourself in this way, it is important to set the scene. Create the space that you would inhabit if you were actually about to physically connect with your dream person. I'm talking low lighting, candles, soft music of your choice, the whole shebang.

Keeping a crystal like rose quartz in this space can also be a great support. My only request is that you abstain from the use of pornography during this time.

The task is to keep your brain clear just before, during and after you orgasm. It is during this time (which sometimes is less than a minute) that your imagination is going to be your best friend.

As you approach the moment of climax, I want you to imagine this significant other. Hold them in your mind. Allow this clear space to illustrate what they could possibly look like. Allow yourself to imagine. There is a moment during an orgasm, if only for a few fleeting pauses in time, where it feels as if you have transcended, even left your body.

You need to seize that moment when you have no awareness, judgement or regard for your physical state or surroundings and you are simply existing on a plane of ecstasy. This is the most powerful and the highest vibration to ever exist; it is here that you want to practice pulling your desires from your subconscious to the front of your mind, so that you are able to flood your consciousness at that exact moment.

This is going to take some practice but it is cheaper and more enjoyable than going to the gym, so practise, practise, practise.

KEEP TABS

When manifesting your big love, it is helpful to think of it like Build-a-Bear – you know those toy workshops where you can customise your ideal stuffed companion? Exactly. In this particular field, there are plenty of outcomes you can experience, billions in fact, so when it comes to configuring the person, you want to take the time to get clear about what you want. I'm not just talking the 'age, sex and location' of the early internet-dating days.

I want you to think about your person in detail:

How do they spend their spare time?

What kind of family did they grow up in?

Apart from their career, what sets them alight?

How do they treat others?

The reason why I encourage you to prioritise these characteristics over, say, how much they earn or how fit they are is because the latter attributes are always in flux. As with their appearance, of course you want certain things to be in place, but it is important to manifest a special person whose foundations are in alignment with yours if not you're going to end up re-reading this segment more than I would want you to.

Whilst I encourage you to spend an evening or so meditating on these, I would also encourage you to get into the habit of keeping a mental log of qualities, so that when you come across a person who displays an attribute you admire but haven't yet thought of, you can simply drag and drop it into your mental 'Big Love' folder.

The powerful thing about developing this mental habit is that it is an automatic injection of 'Feel Good'. When we think about the things, places or, in this case, the kinds of people who bring us joy, we cannot help but smile.

MAKE SPACE

You will be shocked to know how many people claim to be consciously ready for their big love but aren't making space for their soon-to-be reality. And I'm not talking about space in your head and heart, although that is necessary too.

You need to make literal space.

Should one of your desires be to share a home with someone, have you thought about how you can energetically make space for them? It might be as simple as ensuring there is an empty drawer where this person could leave things when they stay over.

And then there is also the power of making space in your diary.

I have a male friend who for two years straight refused to make plans on Sunday. After clocking his unwillingness to meet and knowing it wasn't because he was going to church, I pressed him on the matter. At first, he seemed a little shy, embarrassed in fact. But after some cajoling, he finally caved.

'Listen, I know you love to laugh, but I swear if you mock me, I won't chat to you again,' he said, the corners of his mouth struggling to hold in a grin.

'I swear, I swear,' I promised, already struggling to swallow my nervous giggles.

'I want to be a family man, so I'm trying to get into the habit of leaving Sundays free so that I can be all in.'

I choked on my drink a bit. Not because I found it funny or

embarrassing, but because it was intentional and powerful. He was a successful workaholic who was notoriously hard to pin down. To see him be committed to making space for someone he had yet to meet has stayed with me ever since.

'I know I sound mad 'cause you know as well I do, ain't no gyal deh bout,' he mused, breaking into patois to lighten the mood.

'She's coming,' I assured him, instinctively stretching out my hand to give him a light squeeze.

'Thanks, sis.' He smiled.

He has been in big love for coming up to two years now.

So, while it may feel awkward, how can we keep the vibrations of our desire to share our lives with someone on the highest level? By making space for them energetically *and* physically. Start seeding the idea of sharing your life by thinking of small ways to carve out space to be with someone, and you will be surprised at how quickly it could be reality.

FRIENDSHIP LOVE

Because you really are the company you keep.

When seeking ways to help us live the life we deserve, we can all too easily overlook, and gravely underestimate, the power of our friendships. Given that most elements of manifestation are positioned as solo activities that encourage us to grapple with things that are deeply personal, this is not too hard to understand.

But I'm here to tell you that this is a mistake. The energy of your friendships can make the magic of manifesting come exceedingly easily or grind to a shuddering halt.

When you and your friends' energy is aligned, you can encourage and speak words of affirmation for each other, your friends stepping in when you are unable to do that for yourself. You and your friends can pool your collective positivity for the sake of your community.

As ever, I would like to use a personal experience to help you understand how transformative collective positivity can be.

GET WITH THE WINNING TEAM

I'll begin this story by saying: I know very little about tennis. At best I kept an eye on whether Serena and Venus Williams were dominating the sport (prior to their retirement) but aside from that, how the game is played and won has never been something that interested me.

Similarly, when it comes to the Wimbledon tennis tournament, I know it as when the best strawberries are in season and the alcoholic beverage Pimm's is the drink of the moment. So, imagine my confusion when, in the summer of 2023, it seemed as if all the universe wanted me to do was attend a Wimbledon tennis match.

Due to having a public profile, in the space of a week I was invited to watch various games at Wimbledon no less than four times. Whilst I appreciated the gesture, for reasons ranging from work commitments to childcare, I let brand after brand know that sadly I would be unable to attend. It wasn't until the penultimate invite arrived that I felt a pang that suggested I was on the brink of FOMO.

But, because I'm not head over heels in love with the game, I decided to just let it go.

And by now you should know what happens when you make a mental note of something you wanted, but you aren't obsessed with it right? Exactly. Passive manifestation.

Two days before the men's singles final, the last invite landed and this time, I was able to attend, albeit without a plus one. I reminded myself that I had made a commitment that this was the year I would start getting flexible with my comfort zone. Even though going to places and interacting with new people scared me a little, it always turned out to be worth it, so with an open diary and no parenting duties pressing, I decided to say yes, while not truly understanding what I would witness.

Because this wasn't any old final. This was a historic showdown between a young, zippy upstart by the name of Carlos Alcaraz and the reigning, tried, tested and most importantly, hugely experienced champion, Novak Djokovic. Everyone who had even the slightest understanding of tennis was convinced that, whilst Carlos was indeed talented, the luck that had carried him thus far would today run out and Novak would once again triumph.

Now for those of you who, like me, are not attuned to the spirit of tennis, let me give it to you straight: the atmosphere was extremely white, with a pungent air of elitism thrown in for good measure. By all accounts, I had been thrust into a space that many years ago would have unearthed feelings of inferiority and low vibrational complexities around belonging. But I had committed to working with Source long enough to know that I was exactly where I was supposed to be. Even so, while waiting for the match to grow in intensity, I took to using the 9x zoom on my phone to count how many of the onlookers resembled me, kind of like a Black-person *Where's Wally?* (I got to thirteen.)

But very quickly the uplifting spirit of the crowd took hold and, between noticing when people cheered and asking my host a few questions, I had soon learnt the rules of the game. The short time I had spent researching match behaviour soon seemed like a waste of time; the one thing most YouTube videos had told me was to never shout or cheer. But not only were the crowd cheering very loudly between sets, at least ninety per cent of the crowd were making it abundantly clear who they were cheering for: 'CARLOS! CARLOS! CARLOS! CARLOS!'

It began as a small wave, but very quickly the cheering rolled into such a tsunami that tennis officials were reminding spectators to quieten down as the players returned to their positions after short breaks. And it continued for the next three hours. Every chance the stadium got, they would rise to their feet chanting, 'CARLOS! CARLOS! CARLOS! CARLOS!'

The atmosphere felt nothing short of electric.

Desperately wanting to transcribe the transfer of energy I was witnessing, I pulled out my phone to text my husband.

'I don't know who this Carlos kid is, but he is going to win,' I typed confidently.

'Nah,' my husband shot back. 'Novak is the GOAT, he is just playing with the kid for now.'

I clicked my tongue in disagreement. He wasn't here, so he couldn't possibly understand what I was experiencing.

The law of attraction would not allow this match to end any other way. The way I understood it, in fact the way I knew it to *be*, was simple. Energetically you couldn't have this many people want you to do well, this many people use their very bodies in support of you having your way, and not get what you want.

If the saying goes that two heads are better than one, then imagine the capabilities of almost 15,000.

Because not only was the constant support sustaining Carlos, almost four hours in (my word, no one told me that this game was going to last so long!) it was clear that the consistent vocal support for his opponent was starting to wear Novak down. The few feeble attempts made by Novak's supporters as they tried to match the impact of the groundswell of support for Carlos that day reminded me how important it is to ensure that we are embedded in communities who will positively encourage us.

Almost five hours later, when Carlos threw himself to the ground in utter disbelief at what he had accomplished, I couldn't help but rise to my feet in celebration of a moment that, it was clear to me, was always supposed to be.

I think now is the time to make it clear that to Source, you are Carlos. This energy wants absolutely nothing but the best for you. It wants you to be the winner in any field you hope to dominate. Once you understand that, and get clear on what is best for you, and that you are deserving of claiming it, it is of utmost importance that you start to cultivate friends that are going to root for you with the same passionate vigour as we cheered for Carlos.

It isn't that you can't achieve your dreams if you are your only cheerleader, but the velocity and intensity that comes along with others getting on your team, is unmatched. But, as in all things manifesting, the *why* is one thing, the *how* is another game entirely.

MISERY LOVES COMPANY

When I decided that I truly wanted to commit to cleaning up my act and taking responsibility for my energy output, there were more than a few friends that were displeased with my efforts. Most friendships are formed out of shared interests and/or experiences and there were a few that felt left behind.

These are just a few of the pushbacks I received when I tried to steer certain friendships in a different direction:

'Candice, give it a break! It's not "every day think big"!'

'When will you accept that this is going to be as good as it gets?'

'Cha! I'm just here for a cackle at someone else's expense, not for all this better person mumbo-jumbo.'

The reality is that when you decide that you need a more positive outlook on life in order to get what you want, certain members of your current friendship groups may not be OK with that. The old adage 'misery loves company' is very true. If many of us were truly in the mood to analyse the roots of our friendships, we'd find a lot of them are planted in negative soil.

Whether it's participating in a specific WhatsApp chat that exists solely to roast, mock or bully others, or maintaining an IRL friendship by meeting for a sip and spill of the tea (that is, the pro-verbial bitch) these kinds of interactions aren't going to work for you moving forward once you realise just how sensitive Source is to such mess.

If you haven't already guessed what my first piece of advice is going to be, then I have to assume you've been using this book as a doorstop!

Of course, it's to meditate (literally is always better than figura-tively) and listen to your intuition. More often than not, your inner compass has already tried to bring to your attention those on your team who are silently willing your opponent to take you out.

I know only too well how bitter a pill this is to swallow. So much so, that in one instance I left said bitter pill on my nightstand so long, my primary Ancestor had to get all up in my business. Let me tell you. I had recently started dating my now husband and a few of my friends clearly felt jarred by his presence. They would do things like come round and physically get into bed with us if we were watching a movie (I understand now how problematic this is, but as a 23-year-old who hadn't yet even heard the word trauma, I thought this was simply us being cool); they would tell lies on him and, most tellingly, they were hell-bent on encouraging me to get back with a troublesome narcissistic ex (whom a few years later, one of them went on to sleep with!) Even though Bodé was making it clear this was too much to bear, I was standing by my girlfriends, because guys come and go, this sisterhood was for ever.

Until there was a sign far too big and spiritual to ignore.

One night, as I laid with my new lover, and my friends slept in the room next door, I was tossing and turning when my primary Ancestor, my father, showed up in a big way.

'Dad, what are you doing?' I asked in shock as I stepped into the dream version of what was then our back garden.

'Fucking hell, Cand, you've got too many snakes back here, Kid,' he warned, as he waved a cutlass around.

Shirtless and sweating, he hacked head-after-head off the dream snakes that were swarming around us.

In the real world, in which my father was very much deceased, he was petrified of snakes. This dream was a big deal, spiritually.

'What's killing me, is as fast as I'm taking their heads off, more are coming. You have to keep your garden clear, Kid.'

I woke up suddenly in a cold sweat, clinging to my measly blanket.

'Babes, what's wrong?' Bodé asked.

'Nothing,' I whispered, clutching my stomach tightly. Unbeknownst to everyone apart from myself, I was pregnant.

Then, as if to confirm that it was indeed not nothing, I heard the laughter of my friends next door float into our room.

They have to go, I told myself.

Whilst I don't have the space here to delve into dream meanings, premonitions, or divination, I think it's important to understand that as your aerial for manifestation starts to tune up, if Source wants you to receive a message it will go to all ends to get it to you. I can count on one hand the number of times my father has appeared to me in a dream. This is seemingly in line with his personality. In life he never spoke unless he felt he had something of value to add, so that's why seeing him in that way, even in dream form, let me know how important it was that I began seeking a new community.

Perhaps my example seems extreme, and your current friendship situation is more of a silent vibe-killer. Maybe it's dissing that comes in the forms of 'jokes'. Or the multiple ways of picking holes in your plans, or other insidious ways they allow you to believe that you aren't deserving of the dreams you share with them.

To keep it real with you: in the long run, this can't run.

But, as my grandfather says, 'You may want to take your time taking your hand out of the lion's mouth.'

Before you end a friendship, it's important to assess the situation, because surprisingly my advice isn't black and white. I can't just tell you to cut and run. I've been the friend that has been left high and dry, wondering for years what I did wrong, and I'm telling you, it's important to make a deep assessment as to why you think the friendship should end.

If you know that a person truly doesn't have your best interests at heart and every time you turn your back you feel your ears burning, it's time to dash. But if it's a case of you wanting to change the course of the relationship, or take a rain-check on the negative aspects of the friendship, you owe it to the other person to say so.

Like all relationships, friendships need good communication.

And it would be my sincere hope that if one of my friends wanted to change the course of our dialogue, or check in on the intentions of our catch-ups, I would be offered the grace of being given a moment to understand why these changes will be best for all of us.

If you want to start changing the team atmosphere, instead of opening up the conversations with:

'So, guess what I heard?'

You could try:

'So, what are we hoping to achieve this week?'

Asking questions that align with the highest vision you see for yourself and – hopefully – those around you is always a good place to start.

But be warned, that, as the saying goes, 'you can take a horse to water, but you can't make it drink'. There may be friends of yours who don't want to take action in creating a more positive atmosphere and you are going to have to be OK with that.

As heart breaking as it was, I knew after that dream of my dad that I couldn't afford to be lukewarm about my new reality and, to be honest, neither can you. As I keep saying, ninety per cent of our thinking, programming and messaging happens on a subconscious level.

We need to be crystal clear about how much influence our regular interactions have on our current reality. If most of your back and forth is low vibrational gossip and bad mind-yapping, then you will for sure meet that negative energy when it circles back, sooner rather than later.

It's important to understand that no one is to blame here. Some awaken to the power of Source earlier than others and unfortunately some will stumble through life never paying it much attention at all. But the reality is if you've seen it work for you once, there is no going back. Maintaining friendships with people who aren't on the same page is going to be a struggle, but only you can say whether it's worth it.

Of course, ending any kind of relationship can be painful, and let me remind you that it's of the upmost importance that you exercise your intuition when it comes to making a decision about which relationships need to hit the chopping block. For some of you, that may be too much too soon. If this is the case, then at the very least I would encourage you to dial back the amount of time you are giving to low vibrational friendships, because essentially these aren't the elements of a winning team.

BUILD-A-FRIEND

Maybe you're reading this thinking, *chopping block*? I don't even have enough of a community to start trimming down! Just as we explored with manifesting your ideal romantic love, maybe you need to *build* your winning team?

My advice here is:

Go where they let you GLOW.

For this you may need to seek out new spaces where you can find like-minded people. To do this well, think back to our conversation about vision boarding (see pages 67–76): you may even want to create a mini one just for this exercise. Think about the activities that truly make you feel that zsa zsa zu! Reconnect with the things you most enjoyed doing as a child, or the thing that now makes time pass so quickly you don't even recognise when the sun is going down.

For example, one of my closest friends adores open-water swimming. Nothing makes her happier than shimmying into a wetsuit and being in a large body of water. Whenever she feels off-kilter or like she's having to try too hard to get what she deserves, her instinct will tell her to 'Go where she is able to Glow', which is usually to the nearest lake. Over time, she has been able to strike up conversations and then go on to make friends with people who enjoy similar activities. Recently she went on a one-week surfing trip with two of the people she had met whilst open-water swimming. What began as a solitary enjoyment has now become something that includes a supportive community tied together by a similar interest.

For my husband, it's driving. If he is having an energetic lull, his pull is to driving, the literal art of moving forward is what energetically helps him shift gears. And I'm not talking about the stop-start of the school drop-off; he requires open roads and winding lanes. After a few head nods with other school dads who clearly like their cars too, they started inviting him to car events or days where they all go out and hit the road. Watching him develop these new friendships later in life has been very inspiring.

Whatever it is, once we find the activities that make us feel alive, we can build friendships based on a positive foundation – the things which set us alight – instead of on disliking others or trauma bonding. And that is going to be far better for us and our magic making possibilities.

It is here that I would like to speak directly to the readers who identify as Black. I can appreciate that seeking new friendships can be terrifying, due to the multiple hurdles standing between us, and acceptance and access.

Growing up, it's perhaps likely that you were told by an elder that they 'weren't one of your little friends'. Although this can be seen as just a funny little takeaway dished out to remind us that we were in no place to challenge those older than us, it often stopped us from opening up to them at all. Naturally we craved a space where we could carry all our thoughts and feelings, with friendships being the first port of call. Many of us built fierce friendship groups at school, but when it came time to bring a friend home, we just didn't bother because we knew they would be met with negative appraisal. If you were lucky, you had parents who would grin and bear the presence of your bestie and wait until their back was turned until they ripped them to shreds. But for the unfortunate few, they wouldn't even wait that long:

'You don't go to school to make friends, you go to do your work.'

'Keep your friends outside.'

'You're too trusting.'

'Not everyone is for you.'

I had one family member who just always had something bad to say about my female friends. If it was a male friend, fine. Male and gay? Even better. But when she would see that I was developing friendships with other women, she would, with all her might, try to sully it. It took years (after cutting her off) for me to realise that she was threatened by the potential of another woman somehow taking her place. When I shared this with my immediate friendship group, I was shocked to see how common this was. There was a thread of jealousy running through these scenarios that was too obvious to ignore.

To add insult to injury, there seems to be no reprieve in the professional world either. Many of us don't feel as though we are able to let our guard down in a work setting, because if we show our true selves whilst on the job, it could be used against us. I remember starting in a junior role in a big company. I let out a sigh of relief when on the first day I was introduced to two other Black women working in the same department. Immediately I assumed this was going to be a safe space. As the weeks went on, I tried to conjure up conversation with them both on separate occasions. Each time I was met with an icy apprehension that made it clear that neither of them were particularly interested in being friendly with me.

One day there was an office conversation about where everyone was from. I joined the conversation speaking about my Jamaican heritage and even spoke a little patois. At the time, I felt like the conversation went well, and that I was finally starting to integrate myself and become part of the team.

Later that day one of the Black women pulled me aside and let me know that she thought my addition of patois was unprofessional, and I needed to be careful about not trying to do 'too much'.

I felt the familiar sting of tears, but instead of showing how deeply her reprimand had cut me, I thanked her for advice and made sure to never open my mouth in a group setting again.

So that's what the elders meant.

And whilst their apprehension can seem annoying, I think it's important to analyse the roots of these fears. As a community, we are still working through the historical repercussions that came along with trusting new people. I don't think we need a history lesson to remember how badly things went when we last did that on a big scale.

I spent years incorrectly believing that seeking a new community outside of the one I had grown up in was going to lead to my immediate demise. Only through therapy was I able to understand that I was being fed fear, and that the energy I needed to support my dreams wasn't readily available from those around me, who were discouraging me from seeking like-minded people. My true wish is that I hadn't delayed taking action so long, because embedding myself in a community of friends that is filled with love, compassion and grace has helped me develop my manifestation skills tenfold.

I can appreciate that for some, actually meeting new people, in real life is not a task they can yet, if ever, undertake.

When I feel like this, I am so grateful for digital connection.

Nothing infuriates me more than those who turn up their nose at online friendships, claiming that it's not a 'real' community or as 'good' as real-life relationships. Yes, you will need to make more effort to check if the person or people are genuine, but that doesn't mean that the bond forged between you is any less real. And guess what, Source couldn't care less how the energy is packaged; it just wants to ensure you're getting what you need.

So, whether it's through gaming, an online book club or a virtual knitting club, please remember that there are ways to build meaningful relationships that don't require you to be actually outside or in person. Some of my hardest battles have been ferociously fought on my behalf by my online community. My inner circle call them the Candie Canes. This isn't to say that I'm dependent on my online community to support me blindly, or that I am allergic to correction, but I've seen the power of what can be achieved when people I've never even met in person go out to bat for me collectively. It's one of the reasons you're now holding this book in your hands.

No matter how you decide to do it, the most beautiful thing about attracting a like-minded community is watching the unbeatable force that is **Group Manifestation.**

Now, when I feel as though I have a mountain too steep to climb, or that a cloud that's a little too grey has rolled in, I know that my crew are one phone call, text or drive away.

And this, of course, works the other way too.

While I was writing this book, one of my closest friends decided it was time to come closer to her community. As a hard-working single mum, she had quite literally fled our hometown recognising that the atmosphere was no longer conducive for building the best life for her or her child.

At first, she moved painfully far away, with no one she truly trusted nearby. After three years of deep work and self-understanding she heard the call from Source loud and clear. In order to go to the next level of her dreams she would have to move a little closer to the people she loved.

On paper this move, at that time, seemed ridiculous. The housing market was imploding. Mortgage rates were spiking faster than the blood of a teen after ten Krispy Kremes. The rental market had become a bidding war with greedy landlords only interested in who could pay the most.

'Is this crazy?' she sighed one night, growing frightened by the realisation that all logic pointed towards this being a terrible decision.

'Yep!' I answered, 'But when did we ever propel forward by acting sane?' I asked her, rhetorically.

'Whew, child, that's a word. Preach on, preacher!' she giggled.

'Nah, babes, I gotta keep it a buck. If we're waiting for all the ducks to line up, for everything to make sense, we would still be on Kellett Road in Brixton, singing our shoulda coulda wouldas. Look how much both our lives have changed by just trusting that the universe wants the best for us. Don't pussy out now,' I begged.

'I hear you, fam. But listen, when I drop the SOS saying that I need you to meditate, repeat the ASKfirmations and call on the Ancestors, just get busy,' she ordered.

'Say less,' I promised, knowing with all confidence that the magic of Group Manifestation was not to be played with.

Less than two weeks later, the call came.

'Bruv–' she began. I knew the cadence of her voice anywhere; she was scared, 'Listen, a house has just come on the market, and it's less than a ten-minute walk from yours.'

'Drop me the pin now, please.'

Within seconds the precise location of the house was with me.

'I don't know . . .' she began.

'I don't want to hear the trepidation,' I warned, 'What you need to do is phone the estate agent now and ensure that you're the first to clap eyes on this space in the morning.'

'You're right.'

'Once I'm done writing, I'm gonna take a walk and do what I need to do,' I laughed.

'You know, I don't doubt that!' she chuckled.

I made good on my promise. As I headed towards the house, I thought of every time I had needed to move and how impossible it had all felt. If it wasn't the finances, it was the timing; if it wasn't the timing, it was finding a property suitable. Each and every time, I had hit up my community and asked them to go into their high vibrational toolboxes on my behalf. By the time I reached the house, I was extremely emotional, thinking about how selfless others had been with their own energy in ensuring that I was able to get what I needed. Now it was time to return the favour.

I stood in front of that house and took in every facet of it. I imagined our children playing in the front yard. I saw us laughing as one of us tried to work a lawnmower.

For a few moments I closed my eyes and just imagined all the positive outcomes that came with the growth of our community.

And no, before you ask, I thought not a dicky bird about looking crazy. What my friend needed was more important than a passer-by's two-second perception of me.

Before leaving, I touched the fence and silently thanked Source for what it was about to allow to open up. And then I skipped away from there with an energy that could only be read as, '**This is already done.**'

Later that evening, I learned that my husband had driven to the house too. Whilst on the surface Bodé doesn't appear all that keen on manifestation, when you dig a little deeper he admits that some of my beliefs and tools have rubbed off on him. So, it was no surprise to me that, in his own way, he too threw his energy into ensuring that my best friend had what she needed.

Two days later, as I was excitely getting ready for the sold-out live show of my podcast recording, I got the call I expected.

'Firstly, I've arrived here and man the Candie Canes are so excited!' she began.

'Secondly . . . Fam, I got the yard!' she yelled.

'Argggghhhhhh!' I screamed gleefully, quickly wiping away unexpected tears of joy that threatened to ruin my newly painted face.

'She got the house!' I told the dressing room, whom only a few moments before I had updated on the situation.

The entire space broke out in cheers.

'Nah, let me go 'cause I'm going to cry,' she warned.

'I'll see you on stage in a few,' she sang before ending the call.

I allowed myself to feel all the emotions.

'Well, that's one more reason to pop the champagne!' someone said.

'Yes please!' I responded.

This is the power of getting with the winning team, a group of people who love and support you so completely, that whatever you want for yourself, they want it too. Depending on where you are in building this community and establishing these friendships, it's often hard to believe such a tribe exits and most importantly that even if they did, that you are worthy of their positivity and most importantly, their love. Take it from someone who took far too long to really understand how powerful Group Manifestation is: you are going to go far by yourself, but you will get what you desire so much faster in partnership with others.

HAPPINESS

No one enjoys being sad. Like, if sad were a chocolate it would be that rogue caramel thing that's been at the bottom of the tin for quite a while because no one wants it. But the reality is, sometimes the opposite of happiness will choose you. To manifest doesn't mean that we will avoid experiencing the important range of human emotions, it means watching out for the ones that will kick us onto the highest vibration with haste, so that we can be open to attracting all that we desire.

WHAT IS HAPPINESS?

Research says that happiness is typically made up of feelings of fulfilment, joy and contentment.

Sometimes losing happiness is like misplacing a wallet or piece of jewellery in your house. If you've ever experienced that maddening feeling of losing something at home, then you know all too well the steps that come after.

First, there is panic as you try to retrace every step. You're turning over every rug, duvet and cushion that dares to get in your way.

Once panic dies down, in steps annoyance. You become annoyed with the item itself, for having the balls to go missing. Then you turn the anger inwards towards yourself for being so careless in the first place.

After a few hours or in some cases days, you just come to accept that it will turn up when you're not actively looking for it.

This, this sweet moment of acceptance that is propped up by the knowledge that what you're looking for must turn up eventually, is exactly the feeling needed to bring your manifestations into the physical. That eternal marriage of **acceptance** and **confidence** is the secret sauce that you are going to need to dip into, time and time again. These are the two main ingredients of manifestation.

I have, of course, experienced this kind of not being happy. Now, the interesting thing about happiness is that it has no problem hopping into bed with counterparts it has nothing in common with. You can experience moments of happiness whilst grieving, you can experience glimpses of happiness whilst going through heartache hell, you can even sniff out happiness in a room full of sad.

But there was a period of time when I completely lost all of my happiness. It was like staring into a barrel of darkness. It didn't take long for Dr Lee, the same doctor who had diagnosed me with fibromyalgia, to diagnose me with post-partum depression.

Nothing about new motherhood was bringing me joy. When I finally admitted to him that I was letting my young baby cry for longer than was necessary, it felt like a weight was being lifted off my shoulders. Dr Lee assessed that, unlike for fibromyalgia, he needed to act quickly as there wasn't sufficient time to prescribe anything holistic. It was time for the hard stuff. Anti-depressants.

Happy Pills, as I had come to call them, weren't alien to me. Multiple family members needed them, as did my some of my friends. Although I felt as though none of my loved ones were truly present when they were taking their medication, it beat them drowning their sorrows in alcohol or me trying to talk them out of ending their lives.

When I first started taking the pills, I didn't feel anything for the first week but then, sure enough, the cling film rolled in.

That's the only way I can describe it, you see. Sure, I was starting to feel lighter and less depressed, but it also felt as if there were a thin layer of cling film developing between 'normal' Candice and 'Happy Pills' Candice.

Whilst Happy Pills Candice was smiling more, happiness never really penetrated the soul of normal Candice. But I pressed on because at least using this medication made mothering more bearable. If I had to make the trade-off between 'real me' and being a good mother, then the latter would always win.

And she won for about a year, until the real me got too loud and too strong. She started to poke holes in the cling film and remind me that this feeling I was now so dependent on was literally manufactured.

My version of happiness wasn't real.

I wanted to feel it again. And I mean **really** feel it again.

Slowly, with Dr Lee's support, I began to wean myself off my anti-depressants and find ways to support my mental health and feel happy. In my opinion, happiness in the way it's been sold to us is quite fleeting. It's often attached to achieving a goal – winning the lottery or having a baby – things we cannot do every single day. Working my way towards my happy made me realise that happiness wasn't the mood I should be chasing at all.

It was actually **contentment.**

In doing so, I have to admit that for the past five years, I have experienced happiness every single day.

Now, remember, happiness doesn't need to be the primary mood you experience, nor *can* it be the mood you experience 24/7, 365. You just need to have dollops of it daily. A bit like sugar, a little goes a long way.

If you believe that you won't be content and therefore *happy* until you've manifested the wellness, the wealth or the love that you desire then I have to break it to you gently . . . you will never actually be happy. Reason being, you are ignorantly thinking that it is only after acquiring one of your desires tied to one of the above pillars that contentment will have reason to suddenly drop in your lap.

Newsflash. Plenty of people who seem to 'have it all' are deeply unhappy. And I know enough of them personally to say that with every goal they attained, or box they ticked, they assumed that this, *this next thing*, would be the magic moment happiness found them.

There was, and will always be, a next thing.

Like almost everything I have shared and will share in this book, **happiness is a practice.** You must dedicate yourself to developing contentment as your lead emotion, and the best way to do so is to find it in as many areas of your life as you possibly can, even if you are in the process of trying to manifest your idea of 'better' or 'more'.

Source cannot ascertain that you are trying.

It can only pick up on what is or what is not.

You can be piping hot or freezing cold but for the love of it all, please don't waste your time by being lukewarm.

What I need you to understand is that being happy is the result of practising the characteristics of happiness, the most primary being contentment.

The more content you are with what you currently have and where you currently are, the happier you will feel. And feeling is what?

Everything.

Good, you remember.

I think confusion sets in because people fear that, if they show contentment, it will send out a signal to Source which says, 'Hey, I'm actually quite comfortable with all I've got going on, no need to upgrade me.'

When, in actual fact, it's the complete opposite. Contentment, like gratitude, just signifies that you are so deeply convinced that your manifestations will come to pass, there is no reason to feel anything but good about the present. If you spend your time cursing your current circumstances you are going to have a long road ahead of you.

Remember:

It's not 'Why, me?' but 'Wow, me!'

You have to show trust in what is coming your way.

When you are anything other than content it sets the vibration at 'there is nothing to be excited about yet.' And, as we have learned, what you emit, you attract. Truly nothing to be excited about.

The wondrous thing about contentment is that it is not reliant on grand gestures or special dates. You do not need to be taken on a helicopter ride in order to feel content, it simply means not being *desperate* for more.

Because most of us come to manifesting as a last resort, we often arrive a little worse for wear and, most worryingly of all, desperate. It's only natural. But as I told you in the love pillar, no scent is more off-putting to Source than *Eau Du Parfum Desperation*, as to be desperate for something is to send signals that it isn't coming.

I ain't never seen anybody desperate to pay their energy bills, because everyone knows that the energy company is going to collect their coin no matter what.

Well, Source is going to read your energy no matter what, so you're going to want to stay far away from appearing desperate, even if your current situation would usually demand that you do so. You must believe your manifestation before any of it comes to pass.

Easy for you to say, Candice.

I won't lie, currently: yes, very easy for me to say. But that's because I've worked with Source on over one million ways to get what I want. And by the 500k mark I clocked that **nothing changes before your mind does**. The true tipping point is feeling, believing and seeing the desire (in your head) before it actually manifests.

But in the early days of this journey my biggest enemy was fear. And, boy, was that bitch loud!

A lot like using ASKfirmations, I have found it useful to turn the statements I found my fears were telling me into questions instead:

'This is not going to work out.'

Who can help me can figure this out?

'There is no way I will land on my feet.'

How can I ensure I don't experience this again?

'I have bad luck.'

What can I do in this very moment to start to change course?

I have found that doing this pushes small logic out of the way and starts to make room for big magic.

Now, because we are trying to change our mood and therefore our emotions as quickly as possible, let's think about some of the ways we can get our subconscious working on our behalf. Just like the habit we develop with ASKfirmations, we want to give our brain the space to look for the numerous ways we can solve problems, not fall at the first negative hurdle of falsely believing that there is no resolution to be found.

A way to activate your subconscious onto a higher, happier vibe could be closer to your fingertips than you think.

SET A SOUNDTRACK

I know everyone says they are a huge fan of music but personally, there is little I can do without it. When I was studying for exams, I realised that my revision was always amplified if I had music playing in the background. And this use of music has bled into my adult life so much that I'm currently writing this sentence with headphones in (for those wondering, the tune of the moment is 'Desire' by Cleo Sol). People are fascinated when I share with them that I'm able to literally sing along to music whilst writing my next novel. Although I can't explain how I'm able to do it, I must share how powerful I've found music to be.

With this said, it must be the *right* music. Now, *right* is based on opinion and of course there are a plethora of genres to choose from, but what constitutes *right* to me is music that leaves me feeling uplifted and hopeful – warm, in fact. You've got to match the music to the vibe. As an example, it's unlikely that you would listen to classical or jazz café music whilst engaging in a HIIT workout; you want music that is going to push you beyond what you believe your physical limitations to be. And the same goes for music that makes you happy.

Whilst writing this book it came to my attention that the music genres I was regularly engaging with didn't typically leave me feeling happy. Mostly they hyped me up and made me feel as though I was about to go into battle. So, as an experiment, I decided to curate a playlist jam-packed with more high vibrational tunes that didn't encourage me to rev my engine at a red light while giving the driver next to me the 'Do you wanna have a go?' scowl. And I must say, I have since decided to relegate that kind of music to intense workout sessions only.

Paying attention to the music that I was listening to has been one of the best things I've done to feel happier and more content. 'Background' music isn't just, well, in the background. There is a part of our brain that is registering every hi-hat, snare and lyric and this is what we need to be wary of.

THE 'SCIENCE'

Research has found that music stimulates psychological and psycho-emotional responses which lead to the opening of neural pathways. It was found that listening to sad or hate-filled music (low vibrational) can, over a period time, increase the release of cortisol (remember: a stress hormone) and stimulate the area of the brain associated with negative emotions.

If you grew up in a church-going Black household, you will know that we were always warned that:

'There is power of life and death in the tongue.'

And whilst I want to stay clear of the fearmongering that usually comes as a side dish to religion, there is absolutely some truth in that statement. As you develop your manifestation skills and start to take responsibility for how much is within your power, you will have to admit that you're not just singing along to any old thing; you are in agreement with and affirming whatever the lyrics are suggesting.

Now listen, I'm not immediately asking you to turn your back on all your favourite musicians, but I am asking you to be aware. From time to time, I still engage with music that, at its core, can only be described as violent, vulgar or sometimes a hypnotic combination of the two, but I understand that not only is there a time and a place for such a soundtrack, for my subconscious there is also a time limit. That is not the music I should be engaging with ninety per cent of the time.

So go ahead and have a good spring clean of your playlist. Instrumentals of all genres can be the best way to enjoy music across the board. I would also like to add here how powerful gospel music can be. Honestly, whether you are religious or not, when a vocalist sounds as though they were born in the deep south, can cook a great gumbo and forever be at the ready with a tambourine and a packet of Werther's Originals, then you are onto a winner.

YOU GOTTA GIVE TO GET

You know when the adults used to scold us for only thinking about giving in order to receive? Yeah, I wish they had brought it down a notch too. Of course, you should only give from the goodness of your spirit and never with the expectation that you're going to receive, but I know you don't have time to waste. So, that said, I think it would be bad mind of me to not show you how to hack Source's system.

It is almost impossible to do something kind for someone else and not feel good about it. Think about the last time you presented someone with an unexpected gift – no doubt their smile made you smile. This year I decided that I would pick up the phone and tell people I was proud of them. A few days ago, a friend ran across my mind and I called her immediately, simply to say 'I'm so proud of you.' She was stunned and I could sense an immediate pep in her step. The call – which lasted no longer than two minutes – also made my entire demeanour change for the better.

Giving anything, but especially the thing that you feel you are lacking is a sure-fire way to activate movement up the manifestation chain of command.

For years I struggled to be as maternal as I knew I desired to be.

As a child and as an adult my metaphorical buckets of maternal care, support and love continuously showed up empty. During my own motherhood journey, I spent years focusing on what I hadn't been given in that area instead of leaning into the power of **giving** what I so desperately desired. With time, I have learned that really showing my children care, acceptance and grace has come back to me like a boomerang from the most unexpected places. When I had to have my dental work recently, I was, on account of having had dry socket before, extremely scared of the dentist. But on this particular day, Source gave me the most mothering dentist. She gently stroked my arm and talked me through every step. She dried my tears with a tissue whilst telling me how much of a good job I was doing. Sure, she wasn't my mother, but she could sense my need to be mothered in that moment, and I will never forget her. Whilst I don't pour love into my children or the people I teach with the expectation of receiving the same support back, it's never a surprise when I'm met with that energy when I need it most. Because I get what I give.

Sometimes you will feel so depleted that you won't want to give or show love – but that is when it is most imperative that you do. You don't want to attract more of the same.

As ever, giving need not be a grand, purse-stretching gesture. It could be overhearing that one of the parents at the school gates needs help with pick up and you offer to pitch in. It could be waiving your usual fee in order to help a friend with a specific skill that you have. It could be bringing in a neighbour's bin.

Even small and simple acts of giving are quick ways to trigger happiness in both you and the recipient. When you're met with a genuine, happy response to an offer of kindness, it sends the signal to Source that they should really replenish you with more of what you're giving out. If you're doing well with your abundance, Source will see it as their duty to never let your well run dry. So get to giving in any small way that you can.

COMPARISON IS THE THIEF OF CONTENTMENT

As a home-loving Pisces who gets more invites than she can shake a stick at, please know, it's never, ever, as good as it looks. Early in my career I would pull my metaphorical hair out when I had seemingly been left off a guestlist or when a bitchy PR person iced me out of an event that everyone else seemed to think was the hottest in town. Oh, your girl ran herself ragged with that good old FOMO. Until I started to go to more things and just felt kind of embarrassed at how much I had inflated this situation to be so grand and life-changing in my head.

I had wasted so much time comparing my social life to that of my peers that my Dutch pot of contentment was being eaten empty, much like how I would rob oxtail from my grandmother's stove back in the day.

Even at your lowest, someone is getting neckache from looking up at you.

I think it will come as no surprise that I believe the biggest culprit of this is social media. As I've mentioned before, never before have we been privy to so many people's *edited, curated photoshopped* lives.

Back in the day, all we could do was clock when our neighbour upgraded their car or was the first to mow their lawn come spring. Now we are bombarded daily with the perceived wins of others, and this is having a detrimental effect on how content we are with our own lives.

So let's state the obvious: I'm going to need you to step away from your phone. I appreciate that we are all addicted to our devices and so asking you to go cold turkey may be too much too soon. But I will need you to commit to spending less time consuming the lives of thousands, if not millions, of strangers if, at the end of each session, you don't want to feel as though your life is not up to par.

I am, of course, speaking from experience. With a prominent public profile, I can be especially guilty of thinking that my peers are light years ahead and I've been 'left behind'. So, earlier this year, I decided to cull my 'following' list on Instagram by over half, and I am now toying with the idea of following no one at all. Not because I'm better than anyone else, but because my habit of consumption has a detrimental effect on how I create. And I don't care if you're a stay-at-home parent or the CEO of a Fortune 500 company, the amount of content you consume not only has an effect on how and what you create, but ultimately, your contentment.

THE 'SCIENCE'

Most social media platforms are designed to ignite your neuro-cognitive reward system with a dopamine hit not dissimilar to eating protein-rich food or winning a prize. These apps have been designed to be addictive, because your attention and the time you spend on them are valuable currency to the app's owners. That feeling that the next piece of content will be life-changing or the next video will make your day better is what keeps you hanging on.

When it comes to tools that you can use to help crunch the time you spend consuming other people's lives and triumphs, there are a plethora of apps available that can 'lock' the social media platform you lose the most time to.

As I suggested in the wellness pillar, you want to develop the habit of not interacting with your phone before you've checked in with yourself first thing in the morning. Remember to implement the Soft Stir, the Gratitude Greeting and, where possible, allow yourself to be Nurtured by Nature before allowing your moods to be disrupted by the opinions and actions of others. This part of contentment is completely within your control, you just have to remember to action it. In the early days, you will forget. You will keep reaching for your phone and opening apps simply out of reflex. But the moment you catch yourself, hit a quick factory reset in your mind and start again. Give yourself grace.

UNLOCK YOUR INNER CHILD

When it comes to manifesting happiness, this couldn't be more important.

When you were a child, you did things just for the sake of doing them. There was usually no reward attached and there definitely wasn't a pay rise involved.

You investigated and, most importantly, played because in your mind there was no reason not to. Within the safety boundaries set by your parents, there is a high probability that you engaged with any and everything, without fear of judgement or the overwhelming pressure that your activities had to amount to 'something' that others deemed of value.

As we grow up we are told that our inner child must be locked away. The 'real' world that wants you to be of use to its capitalist structure has no use for your hobbies or daydreaming and so we are essentially shamed into acting as though we don't need or desire to *play*.

Candice, I don't have time to play.

My dear, you're going to have to find it. One of the best and obviously most fun ways to manifest more happiness, joy and contentment is to **play**. Now, this doesn't mean heading to the local kiddie park and bullying a child off the seesaw (although personally one of the things I enjoy most is to spend time on a swing – especially if I'm not with my children). It means following what your intuition is instructing you to do.

You may find you need to meditate in order to gain clarity around what it is your inner child desires. Because for many of us, especially if you are from the Black community, adultification and the mature roles and duties we were expected to carry out took precedence over play even when we *were* children.

Most Saturdays myself and my friends raised in West Indian

214

households were violently woken out of our sleep with the sound-track being some kind of ska, rare groove or old school reggae.

'Get up and clean this house! You think all you're going to do is laze about all day? No sah, yuh haffi get these tings done,' was usu-ally the gist of the first words we heard.

This isn't to say that encouraging children to do chores or take part in household duties isn't imperative to raising well-rounded children, but in my house, and that of many of my friends, cleaning was prioritised over creativity, and responsibility always had to come before rest. The backlash of this is that many of us, particu-larly Black women, not only have no idea what their inner child desires, we feel guilty for taking the time out to find out what that could possibly be.

Earlier this year I made a video where I admitted that for years, when I heard my husband's car approaching, if I was relaxing, I would immediately jump up and act as if I were busy doing some-thing. He was horrified when he heard this and was worried that he had somehow made me feel as though I wasn't allowed to loaf around in my own home. I had to help us both understand that this was a habit developed in childhood, as young girls like me were con-stantly hustled to be either in the kitchen cooking, or cleaning the house. To relax was to be bone idle and that wasn't accepted. The response to that video from many Black women was the same. We continue to punish ourselves for seeking rest.

So, where our white counterparts may be quick to action the things that brings that version of themselves the most joy, it may take us a little longer to unearth what has been hidden.

THE PRACTICE: **USING CRYSTALS**

A great way to manifest the desires of your inner child is to use crystals, either holding specific crystals while meditating or sleeping with them under your pillow. I have found asking a question or requesting the assistance of a specific crystal added oomph to my manifesting. One of the most popular crystals used in this scenario is the Inner Child quartz (also referred to as the 'Bridge Crystal'); the shape of it represents the inner child within.

Blue lace agate can be especially helpful, as this crystal is linked to opening up the throat chakra. In eastern medicine, chakras are the energy centres of the body, with the throat chakra linked particularly to self-expression. 'Kids should be seen and not heard' was a regular adage in many Black households, meaning many of us were denied clearing this chakra when we were children. This crystal can help support free-flowing communication and feeling confident in having our voice heard.

Amethyst is my favourite crystal of all, as I see it as a necessary all-rounder. Its properties encourage calmness, healing and – wait for it – contentment!

BIRDS OF A FEATHER SMILE TOGETHER

It is not possible to manifest happiness whilst constantly engaging with people who think all rainbows do is block the view of the clouds. Similar to the conversations we had in the love pillar, your inner circle need to be supportive of the happiness you are trying to manifest. We've talked about finding friends who believe you are worthy of being happy, but your family are the ones you don't get to choose. In fact, the more you lean into this new version of you, it's really your family that is most likely to take umbrage.

Many of them won't like it and they will work so hard to keep you 'in your place' (which is often, in their minds, below them) that you would think they were getting paid to do so. Try not to take it too personally. You may find it necessary to limit time spent with certain family members in order to not bring your vibration crashing down. But no matter what you do, do not dim your light for anybody. If your newfound way of being pisses anyone off, that's a them-problem, not a you-problem.

Do not let them throw you off track.

Now you have decided you want to take charge in manifesting more happiness in your life, you have to be ready to study the atmospheres of which you are a part. Perhaps before, when you incorrectly believed that 'this was your lot', or that you were simply 'unlucky', you weren't aware of how low vibrational your interactions with specific family members actually were. This can certainly have a knock-on effect on how happy you feel you are entitled to be; as we saw on pages 184–5, misery loves company.

Now, don't get your knickers in a twist; there is no need to cut your family loose immediately, but you are going to have to be persistent at trying to realign the group energy.

Dependent upon where your family members are in their lives, you can use tools from Part 1 that will be beneficial to your entire community.

How about having a group vision-boarding session? Having a positive focus is a great way to encourage even the most pessimistic in a group to be positive about the dreams and desires they have for themselves.

But remember, just as you cannot commit to bettering your life until you are truly ready, it's the same for those closest to you. If the sensible ones are inspired by the changes you are making in your life, they will also want some of whatever you're doing too. Others, as badly as you may want it for them, may not be ready.

But you know I stand on business when it comes to being real and I can't possibly highlight the rewards without warning you of the risks.

Not everyone wants you to win.

Think back to my stadium analogy in the love pillar.

To some, watching you claim your happy and be genuinely content is going to irk them no end. It is likely you all grew up together, so you're cut from the same cloth (so to speak). In their minds they have allowed their situations to be pre-determined and controlled; they are comfortable with believing that everything happens *to* them and they are powerless to effect any change that re-routes the course of their life. They aren't entirely to blame for this. There are a multitude of systems and frameworks in place that work 24/7 to make them believe it's true.

It can often seem impossible to think it could be any other way.

But since you decided to read this book, you have decided there is.

Because I'm guessing, if you've read this book, that you've already heard the call – albeit just a tiny whisper – that it doesn't and will not be that way for you.

As someone who had to accept that there is a grieving process that comes with unlocking the life I deserve, I want to reiterate to you how important you are. How worthy you are of defining your life on your terms.

You've got the key.

Unlock the door.

And run like hell towards the version of yourself that you know already exists.

POSTSCRIPT

I've reached the end of sharing all that I know about manifesting, but I'll excitedly admit that my own journey with creating the life I deserve is far from finished. And yours is just beginning.

As if to remind me of my next chapter, I just received a DM from someone. I don't know them, but I've been public enough with my desires for them to have sent me an image of a Black family, sitting on the steps of their brownstone in Brooklyn.

'This will be you and your family soon!' the message reads.

As I screenshot it to add to my image folder simply titled 'Life in NYC', I smile and nod in agreement. That's group manifestation at work right there. See, even if that person doesn't know about the things I told you, or they aren't ready to believe the things I've shared, it doesn't matter. Their intention is to see me where I've seen myself.

And I have seen her.

At the beginning of 2023, I logged onto a Zoom that was all about intention-setting and meditation, led by one of my favourite teachers and writers, Rachel Cargle. As part of this ninety-minute session, she encouraged the attendees to write about the desires they had for that new year and the intention they had for their lives. Everyone on the call was at different points in their manifesting journey, but the power behind the call that pulled us together from all over the world could be felt by all.

In the middle of the session, Rachel announced she would be leading us in a guided mediation, and she invited us all to close our eyes.

'I want you to look down on yourself now, see yourself from a bird's eye view.'

There I was, legs folded on my favourite IKEA chair. It has a distinctive houndstooth pattern and sits underneath the Velux window of my walk-in wardrobe. It was gently raining outside, and this made this feel all the more atmospheric.

'Now, before you is a light beam that is going to take you way out into space. Allow yourself to be pulled up.'

In my imagination, I swung my legs around this beam, like a nursery child would a see-saw. Slowly it pulled me out of my closet, high above Milton Keynes, until all I could see were lights twinkling like stars. Soon enough, I saw earth in a way typically reserved for watching a David Attenborough documentary. Space was colder than I imagined.

'Now I want you to slide down that light beam and arrive at where you see yourself in the next five years.'

I gleefully let myself slide down my light beam, confident in where I was heading. Sure enough, as I zoomed in closer and closer, a pretty tree-lined street in Brooklyn began to creep into view. Suddenly, I struggled to hear what Rachel was saying. Nervously, I walked up the muddy coloured stoop of an imposing brownstone.

'Damn, double doors,' I whispered to myself, letting out a soft whistle. I wasn't expecting that. The frame was painted a matte black, allowing the gold accents to really pop. Before I had the chance to knock, there she was. Or I was. Smiling at me through one of the glass panes.

She was smaller than I imagined.

'I've been waiting for you!' she smiled.

I wanted to ask how, but all my words got jammed in my throat.

'Come in, come in!' she sang.

She wore wide-legged navy pants, like the ones typically worn by someone who frequents Pilates regularly. And even though I couldn't see the label on her white vest, it sat as though it was of good quality. She wore an almost floor-grazing navy cardigan in the same material as the pants. Aside from a necklace and some diamond studs, she wore a lot less jewellery than I thought she would. Her hair was still as short as mine and interestingly she still hadn't gone grey.

The smell was overwhelming. It was all vanilla and Palo Santo.

We moved from the vestibule directly into the kitchen.

Huge back windows let in a lot of light.

'Sit down, you must be so tired,' she said, patting an oak-coloured bar stool.

I let my eyes make the rounds. Up along the staircase I could see pictures of her children. My children. But they were older than they could possibly be. RJ was with many friends – and by the looks of it Esmé had graduated from Stanford. And quickly followed that by travelling to Asia, if the next few photos were in chronological order.

'Would you like a drink?' I asked me.

'Oh, I'd love a coffee please,' I responded, not taking my eyes off the interiors. This woman was also a very serious art collector.

She giggled.

'We don't drink that anymore,' she shrugged, before pulling a stool that allowed her to reach a higher cupboard.

'Oh – OK.'

'I'll make you some herbal tea instead.'

Before I had time to argue, the familiar sound of a tiny dog tag on a collar pulled at my ear.

'Brixton!' I cried.

I watched him slowly descend the wooden stairs. He was older but alive. And very happy to see past me.

I could hear Bodé's voice wafting up the stairs from the floor below.

I had so much to ask. But Rachel was calling me back.

Time folded.

I was back on the stoop again.

'Before you go – I want you to have this,' future-me said, quickly taking off a gold chain I hadn't noticed before. Attached to it was a small heart-shaped pink stone.

'This is all the maternal love you will need to get here,' she said before fastening it around my own neck. She also told me other things I want to remain just between us.

With that, I was back on my beam, zooming in closer and closer to Milton Keynes before coming into my closet via the Velux window and returning to my houndstooth-patterned chair.

'Now some of you may feel emotional. And some of you may feel nothing at all.' Rachel whispered.

It was only then I noticed I was crying. The next portion of the session was spent with many sharing what they had, or upsettingly had not, seen. I kept my experience to myself. It felt too precious to share.

Until now.

That guided meditation reminded me of not only how powerful I am but also how much say I have in all of this. But it also reminded me of how important **feeling** is. If I know, without doubt, that this version of myself I met in a guided meditation really does exist, I will ask of you what I asked of myself.

How would you feel if you had already arrived at that version of yourself?

Where would you go?

What conversations would you have?

How would you feel?

You see, given all that I've learned about manifesting, I know that I'm being offered another sheet of paper, one that I can decorate in any way I see fit, if only I believe that I have all the tools I need.

And I don't only believe. I know.

I know I'm worthy of living the life that I deserve.

And so are you.

ACKNOWLEDGEMENTS

Interestingly, at the time of writing these acknowledgements I feel more pressed and stretched than I have been in a long while. So, taking my own advice, I would like to thank God even whilst being tested. And I also would like to prematurely congratulate myself in advance for having overcome these current trying times and for finally allowing myself to fully embrace my life's purpose.

To my wonderful husband, Bodé, thank you for having faith in a road that you are only able envision through my description and still trusting my vision implicitly. Forever the much-needed logic to my magic.

Essie & RJ! Thank you both for having the patience to share your mummy with the world. I want you to know how lucky you both are to hear from a parent in this way. Work like this allows me to guide you from this life and beyond.

To Remi Sade, thank you for standing on business time and again.

To Ngoni, thank you for being part of the inner circle.

To Shea and Steven, I cannot communicate how lucky I feel to have you all become family.

Sham Sham – from nursery to New York – thank you for being there.

Man like Kevin Morosky. Thank you for protecting me and encouraging me to bring all of myself to every room regardless of the notion of respectability politics.

Leon! TPGNS!!!!!!!! LOL. In all seriousness, your friendship has been one of the best things to happen to me in a while. Thank you for always being ready to do what needs to be done.

Dain! There aren't enough pages here for me to illustrate how working with you on not only my physical development but, most importantly, my spiritual development has been a lamp that has kept the idea of *Manifest(o)* burning even in the darkest times.

To my WME family, thank you for helping me remember who I am.

Victoria Millar, they say a writer is only as good as their editor and you are a diamond. You have taken the challenge of editing *Manifest(o)* in your stride, and you have been instrumental in helping me take my ideas about this work from instinct to ink. Thank you.

To my wonderful supporters, readers or 'Candie Canes' as my husband calls you. Thank you for being courageous enough to support a woman and her work that most often the world would like to ignore or put on mute. Your support over the years has been unwavering and it has been the wind beneath my wings even when situations have tried to weigh me down. Together we soar.

ACKNOWLEDGEMENTS

Finally, speaking of trying times, I would like to use this space to acknowledge the people of Gaza. At the time of writing, what I am bearing witness to can be reported as nothing less than gargantuan efforts to completely erase the people of Palestine.

I see books as a way to etch thoughts and feelings into time, like a time capsule for those reading in the future so they can glean how we once felt about what, we hope, will have passed. So here I want to say that freedom is a birthright. Liberation should not be earned through loss of blood, limb or life – it should be a given. It's all that is required of humanity. None of us are free until we all are.